INSPECTOR GENERAL
DEPARTMENT OF DEFENSE
400 ARMY NAVY DRIVE
ARLINGTON, VIRGINIA 22202–4704

I0440890

INSPECTOR GENERAL INSTRUCTION 4100.33

GOVERNMENT PURCHASE CARD PROGRAM

August 31, 2009

INSPECTOR GENERAL INSTRUCTION 4100.33

GOVERNMENT PURCHASE CARD PROGRAM

FOREWORD

This Instruction provides policies, procedures, guidelines, and program responsibilities for the Department of Defense Office of Inspector General Government Purchase Card Program.

The office of primary responsibility for this Instruction is the Administration and Logistics Services Directorate. This Instruction is effective immediately.

FOR THE INSPECTOR GENERAL:

Stephen D. Wilson
Assistant Inspector General
for Administration and Management

18 Appendices

GOVERNMENT PURCHASE CARD PROGRAM

TABLE OF CONTENTS

Paragraph   **Page**

CHAPTER 1. GENERAL

CHAPTER 2. ESTABLISHING ACCOUNTS

CHAPTER 3. PURCHASES

CHAPTER 4. ACCOUNT RECONCILIATION

CHAPTER 5. ACCOUNT MAINTENANCE

CHAPTER 6. ACCOUNT REVIEWS AND AUDITS

CHAPTER 7. QUESTIONABLE PURCHASES

CHAPTER 8. LIABILITY AND PENALITIES

APPENDICES

APPENDICES (cont'd)

CHAPTER 1
GENERAL

A.   Purpose. This Instruction provides policies and procedures, and assigns responsibilities for the administration and use of the Government Purchase Card (GPC) Program to acquire supplies and services for Official Government, *mission essential* purposes in support of the Department of Defense Office of Inspector General (DoD OIG). *Mission essential is defined as supply and service requirements that are necessary to perform daily and direct job functions.*

B.   References. See Appendix A.

C.   Acronyms. See Appendix B.

D.   Definitions. See Appendix C.

E.   Cancellation. This Instruction supersedes IGDINST 4100.33, *Governmentwide Commercial Purchase Card Program*, dated July 21, 2003.

F.   Applicability. This Instruction applies to the Office of Inspector General and the DoD IG Components, hereafter referred to collectively as the OIG Components.

G.   Background. The first GPC contract was awarded by the General Services Administration (GSA) in 1989 and the DoD entered the program at the time. The GSA contracts with charge card providers to allow federal agencies to obtain purchase cards for purchasing general supplies and services. The GSA SmartPay 2 Program provides federal agencies with an effective and efficient tool for conducting purchase operations. This purchase card usage provides streamlined best-practice processes that are consistent with private industry standards. The administrative savings to federal agencies are significant and the GSA SmartPay 2 Program provides performance-based rebates to participating agencies.

H.   Department of Defense Policy. The Joint Purchase Card Program Management Office is responsible for the oversight of the DoD GPC Program. The DoD GPC Program supports the acquisition reform and financial management objectives of the Congress and the Deputy Secretary of Defense.

I.   Office of Inspector General Policy. The OIG GPC Program is established under the authority provided in the Memorandum of Understanding with Contracting Center of Excellence (CCE), reference (a). The OIG GPC Program shall support the OIG Strategic Goal 3 to *improve the efficiency and effectiveness of OIG products, processes, and operations.* Procurements for supplies and services to support the OIG mission must be processed in accordance with (IAW) applicable laws and regulations, delegation of authority memorandums, and this Instruction.

J.   Office of Administration and Management Policy. The OIG GPC Program is administered by the Administration and Logistics Support Directorate (ALSD). The ALSD oversight shall support the Office of Administration and Management (OA&M) Strategic Goal 4 to *provide cost effective, timely, and accurate administrative and logistical support to all DoD OIG employees.* The ALSD shall implement proper controls to monitor for and prevent fraud, waste, and abuse in the procurement of supplies and services.

K. Responsibilities

1. The **Inspector General** shall establish an OIG GPC Program. Program implementation and oversight is delegated to the OA&M.

2. The **Assistant Inspector General (AIG) for A&M** is the **Program Director** and oversees the OIG GPC Program and directs its implementation by the ALSD.

3. The **Director, ALSD** shall:

  a. Assign specific program responsibilities to the Administrative Services Division (ASD).

  b. Serve as the approval authority (Appointing Official) for all appointment actions pertaining to Cardholder, Convenience Checkwriter, and Billing Official accounts.

  c. Ensure internal controls and reviews are established to promote conscientious OIG GPC Program management and oversee corrective actions.

  d. Report OIG GPC Program violations and irregularities to the proper officials.

4. The **Chief, ASD** shall manage the OIG GPC Program operations by:

  a. Assigning day-to-day operational responsibilities to the Agency/Organization Program Coordinator (A/OPC).

  b. Monitor:

    (1) Policy, procedures, and training.

    (2) Appointment recommendations for accounts and scope.

    (3) Account reconciliation and online account access.

    (4) Internal controls and reviews.

    (5) Corrective actions to program deficiencies.

    (6) Questionable purchase transactions.

5. The **A/OPC** shall be the focal point for the OIG GPC Program and conduct the day-to-day operations. The A/OPC shall:

a.   Develop and implement OIG GPC Program policy, procedures, and training.

b.   Facilitate the appointment process to establish accounts and maintain the training database.

c.   Provide GPC Program advice and assistance.

d.   Manage online account access with the supporting bank to establish accounts, process account updates/changes, and facilitate account reconciliation and maintenance.

e.   Be a liaison between the OIG, DoD, CCE, GSA contracting officer, and the supporting bank.

f.   Ensure internal controls are in place at all OIG GPC Program levels.

g.   Conduct reviews to ensure purchases are mission related and properly authorized.

h.   Generate, analyze, and maintain statistics and management reports to detect trends and misuse.

i.   Report OIG GPC Program deficiencies with recommended corrective actions.

j.   Report and assist with resolving questionable purchase transactions.

6.   The **Component Head or Designee** shall:

a.   Recommend qualified employees for Cardholder/Checkwriter/Billing Official (CH/CW/BO) appointments to support the Component mission.

b.   Ensure Component purchases are IAW OIG GPC Program requirements and serve a bona fide need for the Component mission (only mission-essential supplies and services).

c.   Foster an environment within his/her Component to provide positive support for OIG GPC internal controls and conscientious purchase management.

7.   The **Billing Official** shall:

a.   Complete OIG GPC Program training requirements and account application/maintenance documentation.

b.   Approve purchase requests for his/her Cardholders/Convenience Checkwriters prior the purchase execution.

c.   Complete required account reconciliation and submit certified billing statements within the prescribed time requirement.

d.   Execute his/her OIG GPC responsibilities/duties IAW the applicable laws and regulations, his/her delegation of authority memorandum, and this Instruction for approving OIG mission-essential supply and service purchases.

e.   Report questionable purchase transactions to his/her supervisor and/or the A/OPC.

8.   The **alternate Billing Official** shall execute BO duties during the primary BO's absence only.

9.   The **Cardholder/Convenience Checkwriter** shall:

a.   Complete OIG GPC Program training requirements and account application/maintenance documentation.

b.   Complete required account reconciliation within the prescribed time requirement and comply with supplemental Billing Official guidance.

c.   Execute his/her OIG GPC responsibilities/duties IAW the applicable laws and regulations, his/her delegation of authority memorandum, and this Instruction for procuring OIG mission-essential supplies and services.

d.   Report questionable purchase transactions to his/her supervisor, BO, and/or the A/OPC.

10.   The **Purchase Requester** shall submit complete and approved purchase requests for OIG mission-essential supplies and services.

11.   The **Approving Official** shall review purchase requests for approval for his/her respective functional area, as the requests relates to a special authorization.

12.   The **Office of the Comptroller** shall:

a.   Ensure funding for OIG GPC Program purchases is programmed in the DoD budget process.

b.   Budget funds for the OIG GPC Program:

(1)   At the start of the fiscal year, establish GPC baseline funding to the Components with GPC authority.

(2)   Monitor Component GPC funding throughout the fiscal year with quarterly budget reviews and reprogram Component funds as necessary. Review and monitor costs incurred for purchases and any changes to projected requirements to adjust funding authorization during the quarterly budget review process. Other adjustments may be made during the fiscal year, as necessary.

(3)   Process certified billing statements for payment to the Defense Finance and Accounting Service (DFAS).

c.   Perform selected/random reviews of account statements.

d.   Report questionable purchase transactions to the A/OPC, Chief, ASD, and Director, ALSD.

13.   The **Deputy Inspector General for Audit (DIG-AUD) or Designee**, in addition to the responsibilities in para. K.6., shall conduct an OIG GPC Program audit every 3 years.

14.   The **Office of General Counsel (OGC)** shall provide legal counseling as required for the GPC Program.

15.   The **Office of Professional Responsibility** shall receive all allegations of GPC related misconduct IAW reference (b).

L.   **Purchase Card Contractor.** This is the supporting bank, which provides the following services to the OIG GPC Program:

1.   Establishes GPC accounts and issues cards and convenience checks.

2.   Issues billing cycle statements for each Cardholder, Convenience Checkwriter, and Billing Official.

3.   Provides special reports for OIG purchase monitoring and fund control.

4.   Provides 24-hour customer service.

5.   Reimburses vendors for GPC purchases.

M.   **Vendor.** A vendor (merchant) who provides supplies and services to the OIG and is one of the following:

1.   Required source inside or outside the Government.

2.   Another Government agency/organization.

3.   Private sector vendor.

N.   **Freedom of Information Act.** Vendors and others may inquire the DoD for CH/CW/BO and A/OPC contact information. This is typically for vendors to compile listings for their publications. The release of GPC Program officials' information (listings) is **prohibited** IAW governing DoD policy, references (c) and (d).

O. **Clarification of Terms.** For simplicity:

1. The OIG GPC Program shall be referred to the "GPC Program."

2. The purchase card contractor or supporting bank card provider is referred to as the "supporting bank."

3. Approving Official, Certifying Official, and Billing Official are used to describe the same official in various GPC publications and references. The term/acronym "Billing Official (BO)" shall be used in this Instruction for the appointed officials providing purchase oversight to assigned CH/CWs. The term "approving official" refers to an OIG employee reviewing purchase requests for approval in his/her respective functional area, as the request relates to a special authorization.

4. The IG Form 34-3, *Government Purchase Card Request for Supplies and Services*, introduced in Chapter 3, shall be referred to as the "34-3."

CHAPTER 2
ESTABLISHING ACCOUNTS

A.   <u>General.</u> This chapter covers CH/CW/BO appointments. The individual being considered for CH/CW/BO shall demonstrate the ability to understand applicable laws, regulations, and this Instruction, along with procurement methods and standards. Each account is issued to an individual employee (no joint accounts). An employee may be both a CH and CW, but each account is separate and distinct. Note: Contractors are not eligible for CH/CW/BO appointments, reference (e).

B.   <u>Training.</u> The CH/CW/BO has mandatory training requirements to complete prior to his/her appointment and annual refresher training is required. Copies of the training certificate must be attached to the appointment request. The training completion should not be older than 6 months. The following training is required prior to CH/CW/BO appointment:

   1.   OIG Ethics Training. This training is available on the OIG Intranet (online). The OIG Office of General Counsel is the office of primary responsibility for this training. The OIG requires Ethics training completion every year, references (f) and (g).

   2.   DoD Government Purchase Card course (CLG 001). This online training is offered through the Defense Acquisition University (DAU). The GPC Program requires annual refresher training (CLG 004). See Appendix F for detailed DAU enrollment instructions.

   3.   Complete A/OPC developed training package.

C.   <u>Internal Controls.</u> Reference (h). There must be a separation of duties among CH/CWs, BOs, Accountable Property Officers, and Hand Receipt Holders. The following are appointment restrictions:

   1.   The BO shall not be subordinate to any CH/CW under his/her GPC authority.

   2.   The CH/CW shall **not** be his/her own BO.

   3.   The CH/CW shall **not** be a BO for another CH/CW(s).

   4.   The alternate BO shall **not** be a CH/CW and/or primary BO.

D.   <u>Span of Control</u>

   1.   The BO shall not be appointed more than seven CH/CWs.

   2.   The A/OPC shall not oversee more than 300 CH/CW accounts.

E.   <u>Appointment Request.</u> The request is processed through Component channels and the Component Head or designee must approve the request prior to submission to the A/OPC. The request includes the required training certificates. A scanned or facsimile copy of the request is acceptable. The Component Head or designee shall recommend for appointment an **alternate BO** for each primary BO. The appointed alternate BO shall execute BO duties during the primary BO's absence only. If necessary, two alternate BOs may be appointed to one primary BO. The following forms are used to request appointment:

    1.   IG Form 34-4, *Cardholder/Convenience Checkwriter Request/Change Appointment*, (Appendix O)

    2.   IG Form 34-5, *Billing Official Request/Change Appointment*, (Appendix P)

F.   **Appointment Approval.** The A/OPC reviews the appointment request and supporting documentation. The A/OPC shall make a recommendation to approve/disapprove the request and forward the recommendation through ALSD channels. The Director, ALSD approves/disapproves all CH/CW/BO appointments.

G.   **Delegation of Authority Memorandum.** The CH/CW/BO approved for appointment shall receive a delegation of authority memorandum signed by the Director, ALSD. The appointed CH/CW/BO shall acknowledge his/her appointment and responsibilities with signature and return a signed acceptance copy to the A/OPC, (Appendices H, I, and J).

    1.   CH/CWs delegation of authority specifies:

        a.   Effective date

        b.   Assigned Component (ALSD CH/CWs purchase agency wide)

        c.   Single purchase limits

        d.   Billing cycle purchase limit

        e.   Assigned primary and alternate BOs

        f.   Responsibilities

    2.   BO/alternate BO delegation of authority specifies:

        a.   Effective date

        b.   Assigned Component (ALSD CH/CWs purchase agency wide)

        c.   Single purchase limits

        d.   Billing cycle purchase limit

    e. Assigned CW/CHs

    f. Responsibilities

H.   **Signature Card.** The BO shall also complete the DD Form 577, *Appointment /Termination Record – Authorized Signature,* (Appendix Q). The completed signature card is returned to the A/OPC for processing to DFAS. The original is sent to DFAS and the A/OPC provides the Comptroller a copy and maintains a copy in his/her records.

I.   **Training Procurement Exception.** The card is the method of payment for all training requests valued at or below $25,000. These purchases are exempt from the restriction limiting use of the card as a payment method to contracting officers.

J.   **Micro-purchase Threshold for a Single Purchase**

    1. Supplies - $3,000

    2. Services - $2,500

    3. Construction - $2,000

K.   **Account Purchase Limits**

    1. The CH/CW delegation of authority memorandum specifies purchase limits:

        a. Single purchase limit is the maximum dollar amount per purchase.

        b. Billing cycle purchase limit is the maximum aggregate dollar amount per billing cycle.

    2. The BO delegation of authority memorandum specifies purchase limits:

        a. Purchase limits for assigned CH/CWs.

        b. Billing cycle limit is the maximum dollar amount authorized per billing cycle for the aggregate of the assigned CH/CWs.

        c. Fiscal year limit is the total funds authorized for the fiscal year.

L.   **Merchant Activity Codes (MACs).** The A/OPC shall assign appropriate MAC for each CH account. This allows the A/OPC to restrict purchases from merchants who provide unauthorized supplies and services. Merchant Category Codes are provided in Appendix D.

M.   **Activating Accounts.** The A/OPC submits the application to the supporting bank for activation. The supporting bank usually processes the application within 1 business day.

Account codes are located in Appendix E. The A/OPC notifies the Comptroller of all account activation.

1.   The CH/CW typically receives the card/convenience checks within 7-10 calendar days after the application is submitted to the A/OPC. The CH/CW activates his/her account by acknowledging receipt (calling the toll free number provided with the card/convenience checks). The Customer Automation and Reporting Environment (ACCESS) is an electronic data interface with the supporting bank to provide transaction review and reports. The A/OPC provides online account ACCESS instructions to the CH/CW, Appendix E (codes).

2.   The BO receives notice from the A/OPC when the account is active. At this time, the A/OPC provides online account ACCESS instructions to the BO, Appendix E (codes).

CHAPTER 3
PURCHASES

A.   General. This chapter provides instruction for the CH/CW to procure and the BO to approve supplies and services for *mission essential* purposes in support of the OIG. *Mission essential is defined as supply and service requirements necessary to perform daily and direct job functions*, references (i-k). Employees may contact the A/OPC for additional guidance on GPC purchases.

B.   Purchase Request Forms

1.   IG Form 34-3, *Government Purchase Card Request for Supplies and Services*, Appendix N. Detailed instructions for completing the "34-3" are part of the form. A completed "34-3" is required for all purchases (training exception noted below). Required signatures and information for completing the "34-3" are:

a.   Requester provides:

(1)   Complete description of requirement to include quantity, cost, and manufacture part or stock number.

(2)   Recommended sources. Sources may be multiple or sole source; whichever are the most cost effective.

(3)   Complete justification or purpose as related to the mission.

(4)   Secure special authorization approval, if applicable. All special authorizations must be approved in advance. In lieu of signature on the form, email or fax is acceptable. Special authorizations are discussed in further detail in para. E.

b.   Supervisor or Designee. Individual is certifying the purchase request valid and is mission essential.

c.   Special Authorization Approving Official approves or disapproves. As noted above, the requestor is responsible for securing the special authorization approval/signature.

d.   CH/CW:

(1)   Reviews documentation for completeness and required signatures.

(2)   Certifies funds are available for this purchase.

(3)   Determines if the purchase is authorized under the GPC Program.

(4)   Assigns an internal purchase control number.

(5) Secures the BO approval and signature prior to purchase. For extenuating circumstances only, the BO may approve a purchase via electronic communication. In lieu of signature on the form, email or fax is acceptable.

   e. BO reviews the purchase requirement to determine the request is legal and adequately justified. The BO provides signature on the "34-3" and returns the form to the CW/CH to execute the purchase.

   2. Standard Form 182, *Authorization, Agreement, and Certification of Training*, (Appendix R). The Training Support Directorate (TSD) may use a completed SF 182 in lieu of the "34-3" for training procurements. Supporting documentation, such as a vendor invoice, registration, training form (with proper certifying official signatures), agreement form, or other related material should be attached. The CH/CW may execute the training procurement without the BO's signature. This exception is at the discretion of the TSD BO. Required signatures and information for completing the SF 182:

   a. Trainee information

   b. Training course data to include training objective

   c. Costs and billing information

   d. Supervisor, Component training coordinator, and TSD Human Resources Specialist review/approval.

C. **Purchase Documentation**

   1. Over-the-Counter Purchases. The CH shall obtain a customer copy of the charge slip and attach to the "34-3." If applicable, ensure all carbons are destroyed from the charge slip.

   2. Telephone Orders. The CH shall retain any shipping documents or charge slips to attach to the "34-3."

Note: If the shipping document or charge slip is lost, destroyed, or not provided, the CH shall provide a statement in lieu of receipt.

D. Purchase Log. All "34-3s" and SF 182s are issued a control number by the CH/CW. The purchase request with control number is logged on the IG Form 34-1, *Government Purchase Card Log*, (Appendix L). The CH/CW may utilize a suitable substitute for the IG Form 34-1. The log is completed for each billing cycle. A completed purchase log substantiated with complete purchase request packages is key to accurate and prompt reconciliation with the BO.

E. **Special Authorizations.** The following supplies and services require special authorization (signed approval/specification by an approving official) prior to purchase:

1. Shredders. The Office of Security must provide specific shredder requirements prior to purchase.

2. Conference/Meeting Rooms in the National Capital Region (NCR). The Washington Headquarters Services (WHS) must approve the rental of conference/meeting rooms in the NCR, reference (l). The requester should allow 60 days for this approval process. Conference room requests in the NCR shall be sent to the ALSD on a "34-3" for processing. The Chief, Acquisition Division (AQD) is the POC for this type of request.

3. Special Drinking Water (delivery services and bottled water), reference (m). If the work location does not have safe drinking water on site; the Component Head or designee shall submit a written statement that safe drinking water is not available. The requestor shall attach the written statement to the "34-3." Special drinking water may be purchased with appropriated funds only when it is necessary, such as when:

    a. The public water is unsafe for human consumption. Water testing agency written report/determination that the work location water is not fit to drink shall be provided prior to purchase.

    b. There is an emergency failure of the water source.

    c. There is a temporary facility with no safe drinking water available within a reasonable distance.

    d. There is no water fit for safe drinking purposes available without cost or at a lower cost to the government.

4. All furniture, carpet, drapes/window treatments, and office furnishings. The approval authority is the Facilities and Space Management Division (FSD).

5. Accountable property items. The approval authority is the Property and Mail Services Division (PMD), reference (n).

6. Reproduction equipment (copiers and facsimiles). The approval authority is the AQD.

7. Information technology (IT) equipment. The approval authority is the Information Systems Directorate (ISD). This does not apply to IT expendable items, such as toner, repair kits, and memory cards.

8. Telecommunication supplies and equipment. The approval authority is the ISD.

F. **Existing Contracts.** The CH/CW must utilize existing contracts in place to the fullest extent. For the telecommunication and wireless services, the CH must contact the Defense Telecommunication Service-Washington (DTS-W) in the NCR or local equivalent agency outside the NCR with telecommunication contract oversight. An existing contract may be in place to secure the required service. The CH may contact the Purchasing Branch Chief in AQD for existing contracts.

G. **Mandatory Sources**

    1.   Existing OIG inventories.

    2.   DoD Electronic Mall (EMall) or GSA Advantage. (See Appendix G) These are mandatory sources/schedules for procurements.

H. **Open Market Source.** EMall or GSA Advantage are mandatory sources/schedules for procurements, unless, a lower price for an identical item (same make and model) is available from another source (open market), reference (i)(2). Purchasing from a mandatory source takes priority over an open market source, with consideration to availability, delivery costs, and shipping time. The source review shall be documented on the "34-3," in blocks 16 and 27. The CH/CW may attach documentation for source reviews. If EMall or GSA Advantage is not utilized and an open market source is selected, the CH/CW shall:

    1.   Inform the vendor the purchase is for official Government business using the GPC.

    2.   Inform the vendor the purchase is tax exempt. If the vendor will not comply with tax exemption, find another vendor. If the vendor is the only source, contact the supporting bank for assistance.

    3.   Inform the vendor that backorders are not allowed.

    4.   Inform the vendor the following must be on the shipping/packing slip:

        a.   CH/CW name (no account number) and telephone number

        b.   Office symbol

        c.   Building and room number

        d.   Street address, city, and state

        e.   Statement: "GOVERNMENT PURCHASE CARD (GPC) PURCHASE"

    5.   Confirm the delivery date.

I. **Computer/Electronic Accommodations Program.** The Computer/Electronic Accommodations Program (CAP) is a TRICARE Management Activity program designed to provide assistive technology to employees with disabilities. It is a centrally funded program that provides the hardware, software, and services to the workplace for employees with disabilities (hearing, visual, dexterity, cognitive, and communication impairments). If an employee develops a disability due to work-related/ergonomic injuries, CAP may provide the required accommodation. Medical diagnosis documentation from a medical professional maybe required for consideration. The CAP cannot buy ergonomic related tools for prevention. The CAP contact information for the main office in Falls Church, Virginia:

  1. (703) 681-8813

  2. cap@tma.osd.mil

  3. http://www.tricare.mil/CAP/About_us/

J. **Official Representation Funds.** The BO must comply with special program requirements in reference (o).

K. **Mass Transportation Benefit Program.** For OIG field offices outside the NCR, the GPC is the preferred method for purchasing transit passes for eligible employees, reference (p).

L. **Prohibited/Restricted Purchases.** The following list is not all inclusive and there may be limited exceptions to the general rule. These items may be authorized as mission essential on a case by case basis. Written authorization must be received from the A/OPC (with Comptroller and OGC coordination) prior to purchase.

  1. Cash advances, money orders, and gift certificates (CHs are prohibited from receiving personal identification numbers from the supporting bank).

  2. Metro SmarTrip® Cards (NCR) and/or similar **individually** issued electronic fare cards for public transportation (***except*** *public transportation fare cards for official government travel in and around the duty station and Mass Transportation Benefits (outside the NCR).*)

  3. Travel/transportation tickets and travel agency fees (airline, bus, boat, train, etc.) to include clear cards to expedite airport security screening.

  4. Travel related expenses (meals, drinks, lodging, etc.) (***except*** *for reserving conference rooms*).

  5. Food and alcohol.

  6. Water-delivery services and bottled water (***except*** *for unique situations requiring a special authorization as stated in para. E.3*).

7. Refreshments for office, meetings, and ceremonies (retirement, promotion, etc.). *Except when specifically authorized by statute for*:

    a. *official representation function.*

    b. *OIG awards ceremony* (Honorary Awards Program).

    c. *formal Ethnic Awareness Program event sponsored by the Equal Employment Opportunity Office where food samples relating to the particular ethnicity are served as part of an education program.*

8. Coffee pots, carafe sets (beverage holders), glassware, coffee cups, tea sets, etc. to include sets/items for serving guests.

9. Personal gifts to include items with agency logo/identification for presentations such as coins, medallions, plaques, trophies, mementos, lapel pins, etc., (*except items IAW statutory and regulatory authority, para. J. and para. L.7.b.*).

10. Organization day items (t-shirts, baseball caps, utensils, games, etc.)

11. Personal clothing and footwear (*except items when specifically authorized such as special uniforms*), references (q) and (r).

12. Seasonal decorations.

13. Individual telephone calls.

14. Membership fees for individual employees to include memberships for professional organizations.

15. Periodical subscriptions to individual employees (*except those made in the OIG and/or Component name*).

16. Stationery-personalized.

17. Accommodating technology (see para. I for CAP information).

18. Speaker fees and honorariums for Government employees.

19. Motor vehicle rental or lease (*except for short term (no more than 30 days) for immediate mission related requirements and fuel may also be purchased for these vehicles*).

20. Fuel for vehicles and aircraft (*except fuel for special purpose vehicles such as fork lifts, tractors, etc., see item para. 19*).

21. Motor vehicle supplies, oil, repairs, maintenance, car washes, accessories, etc. for Interagency Fleet Management/GSA assigned vehicles (*except for material handling equipment, confiscated vehicles, Defense property disposal vehicles, or DCIS-owned vehicles*).

22. Land or building rental or lease (*except for storage rental of DCIS case records*).

23. All furniture, carpet, drapes/window treatments, and office furnishings (*except when approved in advance by FSD*).

24. Accountable property (*except when approved in advance by PMD*).

25. Reproduction equipment such as copiers and facsimiles (*except when approved in advance by AQD*).

26. Information technology equipment,

    a. *except when approved in advance by ISD.*

    b. *except for expendable supplies such as toner, repairs kits, and memory cards.*

    c. *except for a DCIS investigative emergency.*

27. Telecommunication supplies and equipment (*except when approved in advance by ISD*).

28. Pesticides.

29. Weapons (firearms such as a rifle, shotgun, revolver, etc.)

30. Ammunition. Note: All requirements for ammunition should be processed through AQD with a 6-month lead time. AQD procures ammunition from the Rock Island Arsenal.

31. Advance purchases for services,

    a. *except for advance payment of tuition.*

    b. *except for advance payment of periodical subscriptions in agency name.*

32. Printing services. Document Automation and Production Service (DAPS) is the mandatory source for all printing/reproduction services.

    a. *except when a specific waiver has been granted from the GPC Program Director or DAPS.*

    b. *except when the use of DAPS for DCIS mission-essential printing would impede/compromise a case. Waiver authority is the GPC Program Director.*

33. Third party payments or money transfer services purchases, such as PayPal®Purchases and Citibank c2it, (*except when another suitable vendor cannot be obtained to meet mission requirements*).

34. See Appendix K for an alphabetical listing (quick scan) of prohibited purchases. If the CH/CW needs further guidance to determine the propriety for a purchase, he/she shall contact the assigned BO and/or the A/OPC. The A/OPC may refer the purchase inquiry to the OGC.

M.   Split Purchases. Splitting known requirements solely to keep them under the micro-purchase threshold is prohibited, references (s) and (t). Purchase requirements that exceed the micro-purchase threshold must be referred to AQD using eDarts procurement procedures. A requirement is the required quantity known at the time of purchase.

 1.   Micro-purchase threshold for a single purchase:

   a.   Supplies - $3,000

   b.   Services - $2,500

   c.   Construction - $2,000

 2.   Split purchase examples:

   a.   The CH/CW/BO knows the total requirement at the time of initial purchase and it exceeds the micro-purchase threshold. In order to circumvent formal contracting procedures, the CH/CW with BO approval makes **multiple purchases from the same vendor** and the total exceeds the micro-purchase limit.

   b.   The CH/CW/BO knows the total requirement at the time of initial purchase and it exceeds the micro-purchase threshold. In order to circumvent formal contracting procedures, the CH/CW with BO approval makes **multiple purchases from different vendors** and the total exceeds the micro-purchase limit.

   c.   The CH/CW/BOs know the total requirement at the time of initial purchase and it exceeds the micro-purchase threshold. In order to circumvent formal contracting procedures, **multiple CH/CWs** with BO approval **make multiple purchases** from the same vendor and/or different vendors and the total exceeds the micro-purchase limit.

N.   Recurring Monthly Service. A recurring monthly service that exceeds $2,500 per 12-month period must be referred to AQD for formal contracting action. In the event a contract has not been awarded, the GPC may be utilized.

O.   Improper Business Practices. A CH/CW/BO shall not knowingly purchase/approve purchases to a Government employee or to a vendor or other organization owned or substantially owned or controlled by one or more Government employees. This policy is intended to avoid any conflict of interest that might arise between CH/CW/BO's interests and his/her Government duties and to avoid the appearance of favoritism or preferential treatment by the Government toward its employees, reference (u).

P. Conflict of Interest. The CH/CW/BO is a procurement official for the DoD and must be sensitive to his/her conduct with industry. The CH/CW/BO should seek legal counsel when in doubt about accepting a gift or engaging in a purchase action. The CH/CW/BO may not:

1. Use his/her purchase/procurement authority for personal gain.

2. Accept gifts from vendors. Minor items valued at $20 or less may be allowed.

3. Copy promotional items for vendors.

4. Engage in promotional endorsements, but may participate in Government market research.

5. Allow him/her to be pressured or influenced in the decision making for purchases.

Q. Purchase Terms. During negotiations for the purchase, the CH/CW shall determine (as applicable):

1. Delivery date and location.

2. Shipping expense.

3. Damaged/missing items or incomplete services.

4. Return policy.

5. Tax exempt status (discussed further in para. R).

6. Cost savings through incentives (discussed further in para. S).

R. Tax Exempt Status. For purchases within the United States, the CH/CW shall inform the merchant the purchase is for official U.S. Government purposes and is not subject to local, state, or federal taxes. The card is embossed with the statement "U.S. Government Tax Exempt," and the CH shall point this statement out to any vendor that attempts to apply taxes to a purchase. In some tax jurisdictions, it may be necessary for the CH/CW to provide a tax exempt number if requested by the vendor. The DoD currently relies on the card number as verification for tax exempt status. The first four digits of the card (4716) are identified as the tax exempt number. In some cases, a vendor tax exempt certificate is required. In these cases, contact the A/OPC for assistance.

S. **Vendor Incentives.** The CH/CWs shall take advantage of any cost savings, such as rebates, incentives, and any product or volume discounts offered by the vendor. However, generally purchases may not exceed current fiscal year requirements, reference (v). The CH/CW shall take prompt action to forward reimbursements to the Office of the Comptroller. Required business practices:

1. Any reimbursement received by check, must be made payable or endorsed to the U.S. Treasury.

2. Credits must be issued back to the GPC account (no store credit vouchers).

3. Vendors offering any savings shall not be used in lieu of mandatory sources.

4. CH/CWs are prohibited from accepting or soliciting supplies, services, and cash from vendors (no kickbacks).

T. **Fund Certification.** Funds are approved and provided to the BO through his/her Component head. The BO makes distribution of available funds to each CH/CWs. The CH/CWs shall manage available funds by tracking the balance on his/her IG Form 34-1, *Government Purchase Card Log*, or acceptable spreadsheet or check register. The BO may want centralized management of available funds. In this scenario, the BO shall establish written procedures with the CH/CWs to ensure accountability of funds is maintained. Regardless of method used, the CH/CW is responsible for verifying funds availability before making a purchase, reference (w).

U. **Receipt Acceptance.** The CH/CW must obtain a signature for receipt acceptance.

1. The requester or another Receiving Official provides signature and date on the "34-3" or on the shipping document/invoice.

2. If the receipt acceptance signature is on the shipping document/invoice, the CH/CW shall annotate the "34-3" as "shipping document/invoice signed" immediately upon the CH/CW review.

3. If the supplies or services are received at a secondary location, receipt acceptance may be obtained by telephone. If obtained by telephone, the CH/CW shall annotate the "34-3" with the Receiving Official's name, telephone number, and the date received.

4. The CH/CW shall take prompt action to resolve missing receipt acceptance and/or vendor shipping delays. Follow-up action should start on the 6th business day after the estimated delivery date has passed. The CH/CW shall document follow-up actions and attach to them to the purchase request package for further review during the reconciliation process with the BO.

5. Receipt acceptance requirements for the SF 182 are the same as the "34-3," described above.

CHAPTER 4
ACCOUNT RECONCILIATION

A.   General. This chapter covers account reconciliation for the CH/CW/BO. It is a joint effort between the CH/CW and his/her assigned BO to review the billing cycle statements against the purchase records to ultimately certify the bill. The last day of the billing cycle is the 19th of each month. The BO's certified billing cycle statement allows the DFAS to make disbursement to the supporting bank, reference (x).

B.   Cardholder Reconciliation. The CH reconciliation process:

1.   The CH ensures the purchase request packages and purchase log (IG Form 34-1 or suitable substitute) are complete to start the reconciliation process promptly after each billing cycle has ended.

2.   The billing cycle statement is available online from the supporting bank on the same day the billing cycle ends. Each CH has online "ACCESS" to his/her account. See Appendix G.

3.   The CH must reconcile the purchase request packages and purchase log to his/her billing cycle statement. The CH must check each transaction on his/her billing cycle statement for accuracy. This includes validating credits were received, if due, investigating unknown charges and if necessary, attaching a dispute form.

4.   The **CH must certify his/her billing cycle statement and forward to the BO within 3 business days after the end of the billing cycle.** The CH certification includes:

a.   Signature on his/her billing cycle statement and date stamp.

b.   All supporting "34-3s" and/or SF 182s (completed purchase request forms only).

c.   Providing the entire package to the BO within 3 business days after the end of the billing cycle.

C.   Convenience Checkwriter Reconciliation. The CW reconciliation process is the same as the CH reconciliation as discussed above, with the exception of errors and disputes. The supporting bank considers purchases made with convenience checks to be the same as cash. Therefore, it is the CW's responsibility for resolving any discrepancies, such as wrong items, partial shipments, exchanges, refunds due, returns, etc. Resolution on these discrepancies is between the CW and the vendor.

D.   Billing Official Reconciliation. The BO reconciliation process:

1.   Ensures all CH/CW certified billing cycle statements and supporting "34-3s" and SF 182s are received within 3 business days after the end of the billing cycle.

2.   The billing cycle statement is available online from the supporting bank on the same day the billing cycle ends. Each BO has online ACCESS to his/her account.

3.   The BO must reconcile all the CH/CW certified billing cycle statements and required documentation to his/her billing cycle statement. The BO must check each transaction on his/her billing cycle statement for accuracy and authorized purchases.

4.   The **BO must certify his/her billing cycle statement and forward to the Comptroller within 5 business days after the end of the billing cycle.** The BO certification includes:

   a.   Signature on his/her billing cycle statement and date stamp.

   b.   Retain a copy for his/her records.

   c.   Hand carry or email the certified billing cycle statement to the Comptroller within 5 business days after the end of the billing cycle. **Note:** The entire reconciliation process (CH/CW and BO) cannot exceed 5 business days after the end of the billing cycle. Timely submission is required to avoid interest penalties, reference (y).

E.   Defense Criminal Investigative Service Reconciliation. The DCIS BOs must submit their certified billing cycle statements to the DCIS Front Office within 3 business days after the end of the billing cycle. The DCIS Front Office consolidates the certified billing cycle statements prior to submission to the Comptroller.

F.   Late Account Reconciliation. The BO's account is late starting on the sixth business day past the due date. The supporting bank notifies the A/OPC when an account reaches late status. The A/OPC shall immediately take action with the BO to reconcile the account.

G.   Cardholder Billing Errors and Disputes

1.   If a CH receives a billing cycle statement listing a transaction that is not correct, he/she (or the BO in the absence of the CH) is responsible for taking the appropriate action(s):

   a.   Contact the vendor to resolve the discrepancy.

   b.   Notify the Dispute Officer at the supporting bank by:

      (1)   Telephone-The dispute form will be faxed to the CH to complete/return, or

      (2)   ACCESS-Online reporting to the supporting bank.

   c.   Attaching a copy of the dispute form to his/her billing cycle statement and sending it to the BO. The BO shall provide a copy to the Comptroller and A/OPC. The disputed item is charged to the financial records until the dispute is resolved.

2. If supplies purchased with the card are defective, the CH should obtain replacement or correction of the item as soon as possible. If the vendor refuses to replace or correct the defective item, the transaction will be considered in dispute. Items in dispute are handled in the same manner as billing errors, discussed above.

3. Items that cannot be disputed are:

 a. Shipping

 b. Tax

 c. Convenience check purchases

 d. Purchases made with cash drawn from the purchase card account

 e. Disputes if the CH is absent

H. **Tax Reporting for Convenience Checks Issued for Services.** The 1099 Tax Reporting Process is an application created to collect and report payments for services to the Internal Revenue Service. At the end of the calendar year, the DFAS shall total all transactions for each vendor. Non-tax exempt vendors who received total payments of $600 or more for services shall be issued a 1099-Miscellaneous. Transactions made for services using the purchase card are collected from the supporting bank. The A/OPC shall gather this information from the billing cycle records and input the data utilizing an online system. Convenience checks written for service type transactions shall be entered during the calendar year the check was issued, reference (z).

I. **Bank Rebates.** The supporting bank issues quarterly rebates based on purchase volume and payment timeliness, reference (aa).

1. Rebates are issued for accounts paid before the due date (less than 30 days from the billing cycle statement date).

2. The combined total rebate for all the CH/CW accounts assigned to the BO are shown on the BO's billing cycle statement.

3. Rebates (credit) are applied as payment on the next certified billing cycle statement.

4. The rebate credit is shown as *XFER PER AGENCY* on the BO's billing cycle statement.

5. The A/OPC receives quarterly reports from the supporting bank listing all rebates for each BO account.

J. **Absence**

1. CH/CW Absence. If the CH/CW cannot reconcile his/her billing cycle statement within the prescribed time (leave, training, or temporary duty), his/her purchase records shall be made available to the BO for review. This allows the BO to meet his/her certification suspense to the Comptroller. The BO shall review the CH/CW billing cycle statement with the CH/CW upon his/her return. The CH/CW certifies his/her billing statement after this joint review.

2. Primary BO Absence. The alternate BO shall perform the required certification in the BO's absence (leave, training, or temporary duty). The alternate BO shall review the certified billing cycle statement with the primary BO upon his/her return.

CHAPTER 5
ACCOUNT MAINTENANCE

A.   **General.** This chapter covers a broad spectrum of processes for account maintenance. Topics include safeguarding and reporting lost or stolen cards/convenience checks, account updates and terminations, and records retention.

B.   **Safeguarding Cards/Convenience Checks.** The CH/CW shall take prudent steps to secure his/her charge card/convenience checks. The same care and safeguarding that a reasonable person would exhibit for his/her own bank cards or negotiable instruments shall be taken with the Government issued purchasing instruments. At a minimum, a locked drawer shall be used at the work place to secure the item(s), unless further measures are warranted.

C.   **Lost or Stolen Cards/Convenience Checks.** The Government is not liable for unauthorized card use or convenience check issuance.

   1.   The CH/CW shall take the following actions for lost or stolen card/convenience checks:

   a.   Immediately upon discovery notify the supporting bank by telephone.

   b   Notify the BO within 1 business day in writing with signature including the following information: (memorandum may be sent by email or fax).

   (1)   Card number/convenience check numbers and account number.

   (2)   Complete name on account.

   (3)   Date and location of the loss or theft.

   (4)   Date and police report information, if stolen.

   (5)   Date and time for the supporting bank notification.

   (6)   Identify purchases made on the day of the loss or theft.

   (7)   Any other pertinent information.

   2.   The BO shall submit this information in a written report to the A/OPC within 5 business days.

   3.   If the original card/convenience checks are located, the CH/CW shall provide the recovered item(s) to the BO. The BO records the destruction on the IG Form 34-2, *Government Purchase Card/Convenience Check Destruction Certificate* (Appendix M). A witness to the destruction must also sign the form. The form is sent to the A/OPC within 5 business days.

D.   <u>Account Updates/Changes.</u> Process account updates/changes using the same process as for the initial appointment request (refer to previous chapter). The Components shall submit requested account updates/changes promptly and in anticipation of employee turnover, duty changes, and mission requirements. The A/OPC submits update/change requests within 2 business days to the supporting bank. The A/OPC notifies the Comptroller of BO account updates/changes. Account updates/changes include:

1.   Administrative updates/changes to name/contact information.

2.   Purchase type and limit updates/changes (requires new delegation of authority memorandum).

3.   CH/CW assigned to a new BO account (requires new delegation of authority memorandum).

    a.   Required coordination to retain the same CH/CW account: If the current and new BO agree to transfer the existing account, the new BO shall initiate a written request to the A/OPC. The CH/CW must coordinate fund availability with the new BO prior to purchasing.

    b.   If the current and new BO determines the account shall not be transferred, an appointment termination and appointment request are forwarded to the A/OPC.

4.   Deleting a CH/CW from a BO account (requires new delegation of authority memorandum).

5.   Replacing a BO (requires new delegation of authority memorandum).

E.   <u>Account Status (Agency Initiated).</u> The A/OPC may:

1.   Temporarily close an account for:

    a.   Periodic or seasonal basis.

    b.   Extended leave of absence or deployment.

    c.   Blockage of use during a management review.

    d.   Exceeding purchase authority.

2.   Suspend an account for:

    a.   Misuse.

    b.   Fraud.

    c.   Management directed. (employee suspension, security clearance revocation, etc.)

d. Exceeding purchase authority.

3. Terminate an account for:

a. Reassignment/terminating employment.

b. Changes to mission operations and requirements.

c. Inactivity for 6 months or more.

d. Management directed. (employee suspension, security clearance revocation, etc.)

e. Exceeding purchase authority.

F. **Account Status (Bank Initiated)**

1. The supporting bank is authorized to suspend an account when:

a. An outstanding account balance 60 days or more is past the billing date. The account must be paid before suspension is removed.

b. One or more accounts have an outstanding balance of 180 days or more past the billing date. The entire BO account remains suspended until all CH/CW accounts are paid.

2. The supporting bank is authorized to terminate an account when it has been suspended more than once in a 12-month period.

G. **Record Retention.** The document files for purchases shall be retained for 6 years and 3 months after final payment, references (bb) and (cc). The following records maintenance is required for terminated accounts:

1. The CH/CW shall provide his/her card/convenience checks and billing cycle records to the BO. The BO records the card/convenience check destruction on the IG Form 34-2, *Government Purchase Card/Convenience Check Destruction Certificate* (Appendix M). A witness to the destruction must also sign the form. The form is sent to the A/OPC within 5 business days.

2. The BO shall provide his/her billing cycle records to the A/OPC. The A/OPC determines the record retention location based on the circumstances.

3. The A/OPC monitors terminated account balances and takes appropriate action to resolve debit/credit balances. A credit balance may be transferred to another account or a credit refund check may be requested (payable to the U.S. Treasury).

CHAPTER 6
ACCOUNT REVIEWS AND AUDITS

A. <u>General</u>. Audits and reviews are organized processes in which the GPC Program is evaluated for compliance with the applicable laws and regulations, OIG policy, and accepted business practices. Reviews are an informal look at the GPC Program by internal management with the objective of identifying short falls that shall lead to management improvement. Audits are formal program evaluations normally done by outside agents. The audit objective is to provide a detailed written analysis of program compliance.

B. <u>Cardholder/Convenience Checkwriter</u>. As part of his/her operational commitment, the CH/CW shall review processes and procedures to ensure GPC Program compliance. As necessitated by purchase volume and operations, the CH/CW shall set aside sufficient duty time to review GPC purchases and documentation. This consistent review process promotes timely follow-up for outstanding issues and proper reconciliation.

C. <u>Billing Official</u>. The BO shall conduct quarterly reviews of all CH/CWs assigned to his/her account to determine GPC Program compliance. This review provides the BO an opportunity to analyze purchase trends. The BO shall document his/her quarterly review in writing and retain on file.

D. <u>Agency/Organization Program Coordinator</u>

    1. On-Site Visits.

        a.   The A/OPC shall conduct an on-site visit for each active BO account every fiscal year. The BO shall provide billing cycle records to the A/OPC for review (as requested).

        b.   The A/OPC shall submit a written report with findings and recommendations within 15 business days of completing the on-site visit. This report is provided to the BO and the Program Director. The BO shall be given 20 business days to respond to identified findings and provide proposed corrective actions and estimated completion dates, if necessary.

        c.   The A/OPC monitors the BO account for implementing the corrective actions.

        (1) If the A/OPC determines the BO account is in compliance, the A/OPC sends a follow-up report to the BO and Director, ALSD documenting the compliance.

        (2) If the A/OPC determines the BO account is still not in compliance, he/she makes a recommendation to the Program Director through the Director, ALSD. The recommendation may include terminating or suspending the BO account, modifying the BO's purchase authority, removing certain CH/CW accounts and/or continuing account monitoring.

2. The A/OPC shall investigate and respond to all potential GPC irregularities. A preliminary response shall be provided to the appropriate office within 15 business days of receipt.

E.   **Comptroller.** The Office of the Comptroller performs selected/random reviews of the BOs' statements.

F.   **Manager's Internal Control Program.** The GPC Program must be an assessable unit for the ALSD, reference (dd).

G.   **Audit.** The **(DIG-AUD) or Designee** OIG Audit Component shall perform a complete GPC Program audit to include CW accounts every 3 years. The audit shall be conducted IAW standard procedures and a formal report shall be issued to the Program Director.

CHAPTER 7
QUESTIONABLE PURCHASES

A. <u>General Policy</u>. This chapter provides instruction for the questionable purchase processes to determine if a purchase was improper. This includes any use of the card/convenience checks at prohibited establishments or for purposes that are inconsistent with mission related requirements. The intent of this chapter is to ensure that management emphasis is given to personal accountability for GPC misuse and outline responsibilities in the event of a questionable and/or improper purchase(s), references (ee) and (ff).

B. <u>Initial Procedures</u>. The A/OPC shall review questionable purchase (s) brought to his/her attention and make an initial determination if further review is warranted. If further review is warranted, the A/OPC shall request all back-up documentation from the CH/CW/BO. Next, the A/OPC reviews the BO's documentation and determines:

    1.   The purchase(s) in question is found to be proper, no further action is necessary, **OR**

    2.   The purchase(s) in question warrants further review and the A/OPC shall brief the Director, ALSD. If the Director, ALSD concurs further review is warranted:

        a. CH/CW and BO are notified via official memorandum to provide a written explanation for the questionable purchase(s). The Director, ALSD, is the signature authority for this written notification.

        b. The CH/CW and BO written responses shall be submitted to the A/OPC within 10 business days.

C. <u>Notifications and Other Actions</u>. The A/OPC shall take the following actions after receiving the written explanations from the CH/CW and BO:

    1.   If warranted, suspend the CH/CW's account pending adjudication with cause; the A/OPC may also suspend the BO's account. The A/OPC shall coordinate account suspensions through Component channels and notify the account holder(s) of the suspension.

    2.   Notify the BO's supervisor through Component channels of the on-going questionable purchase validation and account suspension (if applicable).

    3.   Notify the Comptroller of pending action.

    4.   Review the CH/CW and BOs' written responses and any other Component input surrounding the questionable purchase(s).

    5.   Prepare a recommendation and brief the Director, ALSD. With the Director, ALSD concurrence, the A/OPC shall:

  a. Notify the BO and CH/CW in writing the questionable purchase(s) was found to be proper; no further action is necessary. Copy furnish the BO's supervisor through Component channels and the Comptroller. If applicable, remove account suspension. **OR**

  b. Notify OGC in writing the questionable purchase(s) warrants further review and provide all documentation surrounding the review. Copy furnish the CH/CW, BO, and BO's supervisor through Component channels, the Comptroller, and the OPR. Suspend the CH/CW's account pending adjudication with cause (if not done so already); the A/OPC may also suspend the BO's account. The A/OPC shall coordinate account suspensions through Component channels and notify the account holder(s) of the suspension.

D. **Determination.** The A/OPC shall brief the legal determination to the Director, ALSD. Next, the A/OPC staffs the legal determination through agency channels, as warranted:

  1. OGC deems the purchase(s) legally sufficient. The A/OPC copy furnishes the CH/CW, BO, and BO's supervisor through Component channels, the Comptroller, and the OPR. **OR**

  2. OGC deems the purchase(s) improper. The legal determination is staffed to the Comptroller and GPC Program Director. The GPC Program Director makes the final decision. The Comptroller initiates collection action, as warranted, through DFAS. The A/OPC copy furnishes the final determination to the CH/CW, BO, BO's supervisor through Component channels, the Comptroller, and the OPR. The A/OPC takes action on the CH/CW and BO account status, as warranted, by the final determination.

CHAPTER 8
LIABILITY AND PENALTIES

A. **General.** The CH/CW/BO is entrusted with public funds and is financially accountable in executing his/her procurement duties under the GPC Program authority. Negligence is the failure to act as a reasonably prudent employee would act under similar circumstances. Improper purchases made by the CH/CW/BO may result in the immediate account suspension. The CH/CW/BO may be personally liable for his/her actions and may be subject to fine and/or imprisonment.

1.   The CH/CW must comply with all applicable regulations, policies, and procedures including local standard operating procedures to support his/her BO with timely and accurate data, information, and/or service to ensure proper payments, i.e., payments that are supportable legal, and computed correctly.

2.   The BO is responsible for ensuring that a system of internal procedures and controls for the portion of the payment-related process under his/her cognizance is in place to minimize opportunities for erroneous payments and to ensure that all procedural safeguards effecting proposed payments are observed. The BO, as an accountable official, shall be pecuniarily liable for erroneous payments resulting from negligent duty performance, reference (x). The DoD shall not seek to recover a payment from a BO, if that BO obtained from the GC concerned an opinion advising that the payment could legally be made, reference (gg).

B. **Purchase Card/Convenience Check Misuse.** This type of purchase may also be called erroneous, illegal, improper, or incorrect. A "fiscal irregularity" results from purchases in violation of a law and/or regulation. The following purchase misuse list is not all inclusive. Each infraction, depending on its type, severity, and magnitude, may be a violation of one or several of the laws listed in para. E. and F.

1.   Supplies and services not authorized under the GPC Program (see Chapter 3 for prohibited/restricted purchases).

2.   Exceed purchase authority.

3.   Split purchases (requirement requires a contract).

4.   Improper sources.

5.   Payments for supplies and services not received.

6.   False, fictitious, or fraudulent claims:

    a.   Falsely representing ones self to be a CH/CW/BO.

    b.   False certification of an invoice or an account.

c. Improper receipt of supplies and services.

d. Using the mail to process a false account certification.

e. Divulging passwords to another employee, in order to certify an account.

f. Ghost shopper participation (see Appendix C for definition).

g. Returning supplies for store credit vouchers instead of having credits issued back to the GPC account.

h. Any attempt to solicit or accept a kickback.

i. Any action taken in the discharge of duties as a Government employee affecting personal financial interest.

C. **Potential Penalties.** The circumstances of each individual case shall determine the appropriate type of corrective or disciplinary action, if any, which may be imposed. Ideally, a progression of increasingly severe penalties is appropriate from minor instances of misuse to more serious cases as determined by appropriate management officials reviewing the evidence in the case in coordination with OGC and the Human Capital Advisory Services, reference (hh). In some cases, the penalty may be a letter of warning for first offense to removal from employment for the more severe incidents. While the merits of each case may be different, timeliness, proportionality, and the exercise of good judgment and common sense are critically important.

D. **Pecuniary Liability.** The BO is financially liable for erroneous payments, reference (x). Pecuniary liability is defined as personal financial liability for the BO's fiscal irregularities. This is an incentive to guard against errors and theft by others and also to protect the Government against errors and dishonesty by the BOs themselves. The BO is responsible for:

1. Information stated in an invoice, supporting documents, and records.

2. Computation of certified invoices.

3. Legality of proposed payments under the appropriation or fund involved.

4. Issuing advice to the CH/CW.

5. Seeking guidance from fiscal authorities.

E. **Civil/Administrative Liability.** Use of the card/convenience checks for other than authorized, official Government business may result in immediate cancellation of the CH/CW purchase authority. A CH/CW acting without appropriate authorization and/or outside of the authority specified in his/her delegation of authority may be held personally liable for his/her actions. Where there is fraud, the CH/CW may be liable for an amount not less than $5,000 and not for more than $10,000 plus three times the amount of damages, which the Government sustains for each false or fraudulent entry or transaction. Civil/administrative authorities (not all inclusive):

 1. Section 3729 of title 31, United States Code, False Claims

 2. Section 3802 of title 31, United States Code, Administrative Remedies for False Claims and Statements

 3. Section 51 of title 41, United States Code, Anti-Kickback Act

F. **Criminal Liability.** Authorities (not all inclusive):

 1. Section 208 of title 18, United States Code, Acts Affecting a Personal Financial Interest

 2. Section 287 of title 18, United States Code, False Claims

 3. Section 371 of title 18, United States Code, Conspiracy to Defraud

 4. Section 1001 of title 18, United States Code, False Statements

 5. Section 1341 of title 18, United States Code, Mail Fraud

 6. Section 1343 of title 18, United States Code, Wire Fraud

 7. Section 932 of title 10, United States Code, Uniform Code of Military Justice (military only)

APPENDIX A
REFERENCES

a.   Memorandum of Understanding between DoD OIG and Contracting Center of Excellence, October 15, 2008 (A/OPC can provide upon request)

b.   Inspector General Defense Policy Memorandum 2009-1, *Referral of Misconduct Allegations to the OPR*, February 2, 2009

c.   Deputy Secretary of Defense Policy Memorandum, *Operations Security Throughout the Department of Defense,* October 18, 2001

d.   Washington Headquarters Services Memorandum, *Withholding of Personally Identifying Information Under the Freedom of Information Act*, November 9, 2001

e.   DoD Financial Management Regulation, 7000.14-R, Volume 5, *Disbursing Policy and Procedures*, Chapter 2, current edition

f.   DoD Directive 5500.07, *Standards of Conduct*, November 29, 2007

g.   DoD 5500.7-R, *Joint Ethics Regulation*, current edition

h.   Secretary of Defense Memorandum, *Internal Controls for the Purchase Card Program*, December 15, 2005

i.   Federal Acquisition Regulation, Part 8 of the FAR, *Required Sources of Supplies and Services*, current edition

    (1) Subpart 8.001, *General*

    (2) Subpart 8.401 thru 8.405 *Federal Supply Schedule*, (Mandatory Use Schedule)

j.   Federal Acquisition Regulation, Part 13 of the FAR, *Simplified Acquisition Procedures*, Subpart 13-2, *Actions At or Below the Micro-Purchase Threshold*, current edition

k.   Defense Federal Acquisition Regulation Supplement, Part 213, *Simplified Acquisition Procedures*, current edition

l.   DoD Instruction 5305.5, *Space Management Procedures, National Capital Region*, June 14, 1999

m.   DoD Financial Management Regulation, 7000.14-R, Volume 10, *Contract Payment Policy and Procedures*, Paragraph 120324, *Special Drinking Water*, current edition

n.   IGDINST 4140.1, *Property Management Program*, January 3, 2007

o.   IGDINST 7250.13, *Official Representation Funds*, May 14, 2007

APPENDIX A (cont'd)
REFERENCES

p.   IGDINST 4500.1, *Mass Transportation Benefit Program*, October 11, 2007

q.   IGDPM 2007-14, *Uniform Allowance, Procurement, and Wear Policy for OIG Personnel Deploying to Southwest Asia*, February 27, 2009

r.   Section 7903 of title 5, United States Code, Protective Clothing and Equipment

s.   Federal Acquisition Regulation, Part 13 of the FAR, *Simplified Acquisition Procedures*, Subpar 13.003, *Policy*, current edition

t.   DoD Government Purchase Card Guidebook for Establishing and Managing Purchase, Travel, and Fuel Card Programs, August 19, 2008

u.   Federal Acquisition Regulation, Part 3 of the FAR, *Improper Business Practices and Personal Conflicts of Interest*, Subpart 3.1, *Safeguards*, current edition

v.   Section 1502(a) of title 31, United States Code, Bona Fide Needs Rule

w.   Section 1341(a) of title 31, United States Code, Anti-Deficiency Act

x.   DoD Financial Management Regulation, 7000.14-R, Volume 5, *Disbursing Policy and Procedures*, Chapter 33, current edition

y.   Section 3901 of title 31, United States Code, Prompt Payment Act

z.   1099 Tax Reporting Program Convenience Check User's Manual, July 8, 2008

aa. Title 5, Code of Federal Regulations, Part 1315.8, *Rebates*, current edition

bb. Federal Acquisition Regulation, Part 4 of the FAR, *Administrative Matters*, Subpart 4.805, *Storage, Handling, and Disposal of Contract Files*, current edition

cc. IGDINST 5015.2, *Records Management Program*, November 7, 2007

dd. IGDINST 5010.40, *Managers' Internal Control Program*, July 20, 2006

ee. DoD Financial Management Regulation, 7000.14-R, Volume 4, *Accounting Policy and Procedures*, Chapter 14, *Improper Payments*, current edition

ff. Federal Acquisition Regulation, Part 1 of the FAR, *Federal Acquisition Regulations System*, Subpart 1.602-3, *Ratification of Unauthorized Commitments*, current edition

APPENDIX A (cont'd)
REFERENCES

gg. DoD Financial Management Regulation, 7000.14-R, Volume 5, *Disbursing Policy and Procedures*, Chapter 1, current edition

hh. IGDINST 1400.4, *Disciplinary and Adverse Actions*, June 5, 2006

APPENDIX B
ACRONYMS

A&M	Administration and Management
ACCESS	Customer Automation and Reporting Environment
AIG	Assistant Inspector General
ALSD	Administration and Logistics Services Directorate
A/OPC	Agency/Organization Program Coordinator
AQD	Acquisition Division
ASD	Administrative Services Division
BO	Billing Official
CAP	Computer/Electronic Accommodations Program
CCE	Contracting Center for Excellence
CH	Cardholder
CW	Checkwriter
DAMIS	Defense Automated Information System
DAPS	Document Automation and Production Services
DAU	Defense Acquisition University
DCIS	Defense Criminal Investigative Service
DFAS	Defense Finance and Accounting Service
DLA	Defense Logistics Agency
DoD	Department of Defense
EMall	Electronic Mall
FAR	Federal Acquisition Regulation
FPI	Federal Prison Industries
FSD	Facilities and Space Management Division

**APPENDIX B (cont'd)
ACRONYMS**

GC	General Counsel
GPC	Government Purchase Card
GSA	General Services Administration
IAW	In Accordance With
ISD	Information Systems Directorate
IT	Information Technology
NCR	National Capital Region
NIB	National Industries for the Blind
NISH	National Industries for the Severely Handicapped
OIG	Office of Inspector General
PMD	Property and Mail Services Division
POC	Point of Contact
SF	Standard Form
TDY	Temporary Duty
TSD	Training Support Directorate
U.S.	United States
VA	Department of Veterans Affairs
WHS	Washington Headquarters Services

APPENDIX C
DEFINITIONS

1. **Agency/Organization Program Coordinator (A/OPC).** The A/OPC conducts the day to day GPC Program operations.

2. **Approving Official.** An employee designated by functional area to approve special authorizations for specific purchases.

3. **Authorization.** This is the vendor process with the supporting bank prior to purchase completion for determining if the purchase amount is within the established CH purchase limits.

4. **Billing Account Statement.** An account statement provided to CH/CW/BOs by the supporting bank including all transactions within the billing cycle.

5. **Billing Cycle Limit for the Cardholder/Convenience Checkwriter (CH/CW).** This is the maximum dollar amount that is authorized for CH/CWs within a billing cycle.

6. **Billing Official (BO).** The appointed BO provides purchase oversight to assigned CH/CWs.

7. **Cardholder (CH).** The appointed CH makes authorized purchases for supplies and services with a purchase card issued in his/her name.

8. **Convenience Checks**. This is an alternate purchasing tool in the GPC Program.

9. **Customer Automation and Reporting Environment (ACCESS).** An electronic data interface with the supporting bank to provide transaction review and reports.

10. **Delegation of Authority Memorandum.** An appointment memorandum issued to each CH/CW/BO to establish account authorizations and purchase limits.

11. **Dispute.** A transaction on the CH's account statement that the CH and the BO do not agree with and a formal request for resolution is submitted to the supporting bank.

12. **Dispute Official.** The official responsible for resolving disputed transactions that the CH and BO are unable to resolve. This is an employee at the supporting bank.

13. **Fraud.** Any felonious act of corruption or attempt to cheat the Government or corrupt the Government's agents committed either by Government employees or by vendors.

14. **Ghost Shopper.** A shopper conducting market research.

15. **Government Purchase Card (GPC).** An official charge card issued to CHs under the GPC Program to purchase supplies and services to support the OIG mission.

**APPENDIX C (cont'd)
DEFINITIONS**

16.   Internal Controls. The manner in which financial, manpower, and property resources are controlled and safeguarded by the regular authorization, approval, documentation, recording, reconciling, reporting, and related accounting processes.

17.   Invoice. This is the BO's billing account statement issued by the supporting bank. An invoice may also refer to a bill submitted by a vendor, such as a shipping document.

18.   Merchant Activity Codes (MACs). The CH is assigned a MAC which allows the A/OPC to restrict purchases from merchants who provide unauthorized supplies and services.

19.   Merchant Activity Type (MAT) Codes. The supporting bank creates a four-digit MAT code by grouping one or more of the 20 Merchant Category Classification Codes.

20.   **Merchant Category Codes (MCCs).** This is a coding system provided by the supporting bank to identify merchant types. (Appendix D)

21.   Micro Purchase. This is an authorized purchase of supplies not to exceed $3,000. An authorized purchase of services may not exceed $2,500 and minor construction may not exceed $2,000.

22.   Official Representation Funds. Appropriated funds used to host official receptions, dinners, and similar events, and to otherwise extend official courtesies to guests of the United States (U.S.) and DoD for the purpose of maintaining the standing and prestige of U.S. and the DoD.

23.   Program Director. The AIG-A&M is the individual responsible to the Inspector General for the GPC Program implementation.

24.   Purchase Card Contractor. This is the supporting bank contract with GSA to provide banking services to the OIG for the GPC Program.

25.   Purchase Card Log. A log used by CHs to manage purchase activity during a billing cycle.

26.   Purchase Card Requester. The employee who initiates the purchase request.

27.   Purchase Request. The form used to document purchase requests.

28.   Rebates. Refunds based on sales volume (payments) and payment timeliness.

29.   Receiving Official. An employee authorized to substantiate the receipt, inspection, and acceptance of supplies and/or services.

APPENDIX C (cont'd)
DEFINITIONS

30. **Reconciliation.** The process by which the CH/CW and BO review transactions on the billing cycle statement and compare to supporting purchase request documentation.

31. **Single Purchase Limit.** The maximum amount authorized by the delegation of authority memorandum for a CH/CW single purchase.

32. **Split Purchase.** Known requirements split solely to keep them under the micro-purchase threshold.

33. **Vendor** - This is a source from which supplies and services are purchased by the CH/CW.

APPENDIX D
MERCHANT CATEGORY CODES (MCCS)

Category	Description	Category Code
A	Airlines/Airports	3000-3299, 4511, 4582
C	Hotel/Motel	3501-3799, 7011
F	Telemarketing Travel Related Arrangement Services (No Travel Agencies)	5962
H	Food/Daily Stores & Drug/Liquor Stores	5122, 5411, 5422, 5441, 5451, 5462, 5499, 5912, 5921
I	Caterers/Restaurants/Bars	5811-5814
L	Contractors	1520, 1711, 1731, 1740, 1750, 1761, 1771, 1799
N	Misc. Personal Services	7210-7211, 7216-7217, 7221, 7230, 7251, 7261, 7273, 7276-7277, 7278, 7296-7299
O	Misc. Business Services	0742, 0763, 0780, 2741, 2791, 2842, 4225, 4816, 5051, 5960, 6300, 6381, 6399, 7311, 7321, 7333, 7338-7339, 7342, 7349, 7361, 7372, 7375, 7392-7395, 7379, 7399, 7622-7623, 7629, 7631, 7641, 7692, 7699, 7829, 8111, 8734, 8911,8931, 8999
P	Medical Services	8011, 8021, 8031, 8041-8044, 8049-8050, 8062, 8071, 8099
R	Membership Organizations/ Charitable & Social Organizations	8398, 8641, 8675, 8699
S	Fuel (Fuel Dealers for Fuel Oil, Wood, Coal & Liquefied Petroleum)	5169, 5172, 5983
U	Government to Government	9950

NOTE: ACCESS provides additional codes and details.

APPENDIX E
ACCESS CODES

ACCESS is an electronic data interface with the supporting bank. The following table provides the account codes and status description:

Account Code	Status Description
T9	Terminated
F1	Lost of Stolen
V9	Temporarily Closed
M9	Suspended
Q9	Closed
FA	Fraud
R9	Cancelled
S1 (Air Force only)	Cancelled

An account code included with account information in the online ACCESS network indicates the account status. Whenever an account status other than "Open" displays, an account status description also displays on the screen for easy user reference.

APPENDIX F
DEFENSE ACQUISITION UNIVERSITY TRAINING

A. **Defense Acquisition University (DAU).** The DAU website is not an OIG sponsored website.

1. Virtual Campus-For questions or problems with DAU distance learning courses and continuous learning modules:

    a. Email   dauhelp@dau.mil

    b. Arlington, Virginia locations   (703) 805-3459 (option #1)

    c. Toll free   (866) 568-6924 (option #1)

    d. Defense Switch Network   655-3459 (choose option #1)

2. DAU Student Services-For questions related to welcome messages for classroom courses and general information:

    a. Email   student.services@dau.mil

    b. Arlington, Virginia locations   (703) 805-3003

    c. Toll free   (888) 284-4906

    d. Defense Switch Network   655-3003

B. **Registration**

1. Link: http://www.dau.mil/registrar/Military%20personnel%20Welcome.asp

2. For **DoD Organization** select one of the following:

    a. *Civilian employee of non-military agency of DoD*, or

    b. *Military Component (for military members)*

3. For **Defense Agency** select *Department of Defense Inspector General (DoDIG)* from the pull down menu

4. For **Sign In Options** select *CAC*

5. Update **Profile** as necessary (correct email address is essential)

APPENDIX F (cont'd)
DEFENSE ACQUISITION UNIVERSITY TRAINING

C. <u>Course Enrollment</u>

1. Select *Apply for Training* on the left menu

2. For **Step One** select *Continuous Learning*

3. For **Step Two** select one of the following from the pull down menu:

    a. **Initial** - *DoD Government Purchase Card – CLG 001*

    b. **Refresher** – *Government Purchase Card Refresher Training - CLG004*

4. For **Step Three** press the *Select Course* button

5. Update **Profile** as necessary (correct email address is essential)

6. For **Step Four** press the *Submit Application* button

7. **Instruction Box** appears on screen with the following information: *You have been approved for CLG 00#, a Continuous Learning Module. The DAU Virtual Campus will send you an email with instructions and allocated time frame for completion. This is a continuous learning module, therefore, no priority is assigned to personnel who apply. This has no impact on how soon you will be able to access the Course. In the event you are placed on a wait list to start the CL module, you will be notified by DAU as to when to begin the course.*

8. Enrollment Confirmation:

    a. Typically, course enrollments are processed within 24 hours. Once the welcome email is received, the course can be started. The course web link is provided in the email

    b. New DAU enrollees receive a DAU *Username* and *Password* sent in two separate emails.

    c. Previous DAU enrollees receive the following instruction: *If you have taken DAU online courses in the past, you already have your User Name and Password. If you have misplaced or forgotten your User Name and Password, they can be retrieved from the log in screen under Forgot User Name or Forgot Password.*

APPENDIX F (cont'd)
DEFENSE ACQUISITION UNIVERSITY TRAINING

D. **Course Requirements**

    1. 30 calendar days to complete

        a. Initial training takes approximately 4 hours to complete

        b. Refresher training takes approximately 2 hours to complete

    2. Score 100 percent on the exam

    3. Submit the Module Survey after the exam

E. **Course Assistance.** The continuous learning module does not have an instructor available for assistance. The DAU Virtual Campus help desk is available to answer questions regarding the setup or website difficulties. The help desk contact information is listed in para. A.

F. **Course Completion.** The employee receives a certificate upon successful course completion and forwards a copy to the A/OPC. The certificate should also be forwarded through Component channels for updating the employee's DAMIS record. For GPC account maintenance, the CH/CW/BO shall maintain a current GPC training certificate from DAU on file.

G. **Refresher Training.** The CH/CW/BO is required to complete annual refresher training (CLG 004).

APPENDIX G
GOVERNMENT PURCHASE CARD PROGRAM ONLINE RESOURCES

Contact Information:
    A/OPC and ALSD
    https://intra.dodig.mil/A_M/ALSD/index.html

Policy:
    Joint Purchase Card Program Management Office
    http://www.aca.army.mil/programs/DoD/index.htm

Purchasing:
    Federal Prison Industries (UNICOR)
    http://www.unicor.gov/

    National Industries for the Blind
    http://www.nib.org/

    National Industries for the Severely Handicapped
    http://www.nish.org

    VA Stock Program
    http://www1.va.gov/oamm/oa/nac/fsss/index.cfm

    DoD EMALL (includes mandatory and optional Federal supply schedules)
    http://www.emall.dla.mil/

    GSA Advantage. Online Shopping Service (includes mandatory and optional Federal supply schedules)
    https://www.gsaadvantage.gov/advgsa/advantage/main/start_page.do

Reference Material:
    CCE's *User's Guide to the GSA SmartPay Purchase Card Program*, FY 2009 edition
    http://dccw.hqda.pentagon.mil/services/purchase_card.asp

    DoD Financial Management Regulation
    http://www.defenselink.mil/comptroller/fmr/

    FAR
    http://farsite.hill.af.mil/

APPENDIX G (cont'd)
GOVERNMENT PURCHASE CARD PROGRAM ONLINE RESOURCES

Supporting Bank:
    U.S. Bank
    http://www.usbank.com/cgi_w/cfm/inst_govt/products_and_services/index.cfm

Training (additional):
    DAU-Contracting Fundamentals (CON 101)
    http://www.almc.army.mil/ALMC_accreditations.htm

    DAU-Simplified Acquisition Procedures (CON 237)
    http://www.dau.mil/schedules/schedule.asp

    DoD Purchase Card Program Management Office
    http://dodgpc.us.army.mil/

    GSA
    http://www.fss.gsa.gov/webtraining

    Procurement Ethics
    http://www.usoge.gov

    United States Department of Agriculture
    http://www.usda.gov/

    U.S. Bank ACCESS Online Web Based Training
    https://wbt.ACCESS.usbank.com

APPENDIX H
DELEGATION OF AUTHORITY FOR THE GOVERNMENT PURCHASE
CARD PROGRAM-CARDHOLDER MEMORANDUM

Date

MEMORANDUM FOR *JOHN B. DOE, ODIG-INV, DCIS, MID-ATLANTIC FIELD*
OFFICE

SUBJECT: Delegation of Authority for the Government Purchase Card Program-Cardholder

References: (a) Federal Acquisition Regulation, Parts 3, 4, 8, and 13 of the FAR
         (b) DoD Financial Management Regulation 7000.14-R, Volumes 4, 5, and 10
         (c) IGDINST 4100.33, *Government Purchase Card Program*

1. You are hereby designated as a Government Purchase Card (GPC) Program Cardholder for the *ODIG-INV, DCIS, Mid-Atlantic Field Office*. You completed the mandatory GPC training program and you are authorized to purchase supplies and services using your purchase card. The purchases must be for mission essential OIG requirements. This is supplies and services necessary for OIG employees to perform daily and direct job functions.

2. In executing your GPC responsibilities, you must comply with the applicable laws and regulations, OIG policy, and your delegation of authority, as stated in this memorandum. Responsibilities are listed in the attachment. You alone, are authorized to use the purchase card issued in your name. Your purchases may be subject to disciplinary action for misuse. If the violation(s) are serious enough, the result may be civil, administrative, or criminal penalties.

3. You must not exceed your purchase authority, unless you receive the Agency/Organization Program Coordinator (A/OPC) approval.

    a. Your single purchase limit:

        (1) Single purchases of services must not exceed *$2,500*.

        (2) Single purchases of supplies must not exceed *$3,000*.

    b. Your billing cycle purchase limit must not exceed *$6,000*.

4. Your assigned Billing Official is *Jane B. Smith, DCIS-Mid-Atlantic Field Office at (703) 111-1111*. You shall comply with your Billing Official's specific procedures to reconcile your account for each billing cycle and complete annual refresher training. In the absence of your Billing Official, your alternate Billing Official is *Amy C. Jones, DCIS-Mid-Atlantic Field Office at (703) 111-1234*.

5. You shall sign the receipt acknowledgement below for your delegation of authority acceptance. Please forward a signed copy to: Department of Defense, Office of Inspector General, 400 Army Navy Drive, Suite 115, ATTN: A/OPC, Arlington, Virginia 22202.

6. This delegation of authority is effective upon receipt of your name embossed purchase card. Your delegation of authority is valid until formally modified, suspended, or terminated, and your authority cannot be re-delegated. You must notify your Billing Official prior to separation from the OIG for transferring records and purchase card destruction.

7. If you have questions about your appointment or any other GPC Program questions, please contact the A/OPC, Administration and Logistics Services Directorate at: (703) 604-9836 or fax (703) 604-5006 or *A/OPC email*.

Name
Director
Administration and Logistics
Services Directorate

Attachment: Cardholder Responsibilities

Delegation of Authority to establish a GPC purchase card account for:

John B. Doe

Single purchase limit for services must not exceed *$2,500*

Single purchases of supplies must not exceed *$3,000*

Billing cycle purchase limit must not exceed *$6,000*

I reviewed the IGDINST 4100.33, *GPC Program,* in its entirety, which outlines the OIG policy for adherence to the GPC Program. I acknowledge receipt for this delegation of authority and I accept responsibility for the GPC purchase card account to be issued in my name.

Printed Name: _____

Signature: _____   Date: _____

Work Telephone: _____

APPENDIX H (cont'd)
CARDHOLDER RESPONSIBILITIES

1. The Cardholder must store the purchase card in a locked container, such as a locked cabinet or safe. If the purchase card is lost, stolen, or fraudulently used, the Cardholder must notify the supporting bank immediately and report the incident to his/her Billing Official.

2. The Cardholder shall complete required account reconciliation and report questionable purchase transaction to his/her supervisor, Billing Official, and/or the A/OPC.

3. All purchase requests are submitted by the requestor in writing. The Cardholder must comply with applicable laws, regulations, OIG policy, and his/her delegation of authority memorandum for the following:

   a. Purchase justification and purchase limit.

   b. Required signatures for: Component, Special Authorization (if applicable), and Billing Official approval.

   c. Utilizing existing contracts.

   d. Mandatory sources to include mandatory vendors for office supplies.

   e. Restricted sources.

   f. Prohibited/restricted purchases.

   g. Accountable property reporting.

   h. Tax exempt status.

   i. Split purchases.

   j. Funds availability/certification.

   k. Receiving Official acceptance.

   l. Account reconciliation.

   m. Resolving disputes and processing credits.

   n. Records retention.

   o. Reviews and audits to include corrective action.

APPENDIX I
DELEGATION OF AUTHORITY FOR THE GOVERNMENT PURCHASE
CARD PROGRAM-CHECKWRITER MEMORANDUM

Date

MEMORANDUM FOR *JOHN B. DOE, ODIG-INV, DCIS, MID-ATLANTIC FIELD OFFICE*

SUBJECT: Delegation of Authority for the Government Purchase Card Program-Checkwriter

References: (a) Federal Acquisition Regulation, Parts 3, 4, 8, and 13 of the FAR
(b) DoD Financial Management Regulation 7000.14-R, Volumes 4, 5, and 10
(c) 1099 Tax Reporting Program Convenience Check User's Manual, July 8, 2008
(d) IGDINST 4100.33, *Government Purchase Card Program*

1. You are hereby designated as a Government Purchase Card (GPC) Program Convenience Checkwriter for the *ODIG-INV, DCIS, Mid-Atlantic Field Office.* You completed the mandatory GPC training program and you are authorized to purchase supplies and services, using your convenience checks. The purchases must be for mission essential OIG requirements. This is supplies and services necessary for OIG employees to perform daily and direct job functions.

2. In executing your GPC responsibilities, you must comply with the applicable laws and regulations, OIG policy, and your delegation of authority, as stated in this memorandum. Responsibilities are listed in the attachment. You alone, are authorized to use the convenience checks issued in your name. Your purchases may be subject to disciplinary action for misuse. If the violation(s) are serious enough, the result may be civil, administrative, or criminal penalties.

3. The preferred method for procuring authorized supplies and services is the GPC purchase card vice convenience checks. This is IAW established DoD policy. Convenience checks may be used if certain restrictions make the purchase card use impractical for mission requirements. The purchase card is always the first choice for making authorized purchases. The convenience check is considered the last resort for making authorized purchases.

4. You must not exceed your purchase authority, unless you receive the Agency/Organization Program Coordinator (A/OPC) approval.

    a. Your single purchase limit:

        (1) Single purchases of services must not exceed *$2,500.*

        (2) Single purchases of supplies must not exceed *$3,000.*

    b. Your billing cycle purchase limit must not exceed *$6,000.*

5. Your assigned Billing Official is *Jane B. Smith, DCIS-Mid-Atlantic Field Office at (703) 111-1111.* You shall comply with your Billing Official's specific procedures to reconcile

your account for each billing cycle and complete annual refresher training. In the absence of your Billing Official, your alternate Billing Official is *Amy C. Jones, DCIS-Mid-Atlantic Field Office at (703) 111-1234*.

6.   You shall sign the receipt acknowledgement below for your delegation of authority acceptance. Please forward a signed copy to: Department of Defense, Office of Inspector General, 400 Army Navy Drive, Suite 115, ATTN: A/OPC, Arlington, Virginia 22202.

7.   This delegation of authority is effective upon receipt of your name embossed convenience checks. Your delegation of authority is valid until formally modified, suspended, or terminated, and your authority cannot be re-delegated. You must notify your Billing Official prior to separation from the OIG for transferring records and check stock destruction.

8.   If you have questions about your appointment or any other GPC Program questions, please contact the A/OPC, Administration and Logistics Services Directorate at: (703) 604-9836 or fax (703) 604-5006 or *A/OPC email*.

Name
Director
Administration and Logistics
Services Directorate

Attachment: Checkwriter Responsibilities

Delegation of Authority to establish a GPC convenience check account for:

John B. Doe

Single purchase limit for services must not exceed *$2,500*

Single purchases of supplies must not exceed *$3,000*

Billing cycle purchase limit must not exceed *$6,000*

I reviewed the IGDINST 4100.33, *GPC Program,* in its entirety, which outlines the OIG policy for adherence to the GPC Program. I acknowledge receipt for this delegation of authority and I accept responsibility for the GPC convenience check account to be issued in my name.

Printed Name: _____

Signature: _____   Date: _____

Work Telephone: _____

APPENDIX I (cont'd)
CHECKWRITER RESPONSIBILITIES

1. The Checkwriter must store check stock in a locked container (locked cabinet or safe) and inspect check inventory monthly. If the checks are lost, stolen or forged, the Checkwriter must notify the supporting bank immediately and report the incident to his/her Billing Official.

2. The Cardholder shall complete required account reconciliation and report questionable purchase transaction to his/her supervisor, Billing Official, and/or the A/OPC.

3. All purchase requests are submitted by the requestor in writing. The Checkwriter must comply with applicable laws, regulations, OIG policy, and his/her delegation of authority memorandum for the following:

    a. Purchase justification and purchase limit.

    b. Required signatures for: Component, Special Authorization (if applicable), and Billing Official approval.

    c. Utilizing existing contracts.

    d. Mandatory sources to include mandatory vendors for office supplies.

    e. Restricted sources.

    f. Prohibited/restricted purchases.

    g. Accountable property reporting.

    h. Tax exempt status.

    i. Split purchases.

    j. Funds availability/certification.

    k. Receiving Official acceptance.

    l. Account reconciliation.

    m. Resolving disputes and processing credits.

    n. Records retention.

    o. Reviews and audits to include corrective action.

APPENDIX J
DELEGATION OF AUTHORITY FOR THE GOVERNMENT PURCHASE CARD
PROGRAM-BILLING OFFICIAL

Date

MEMORANDUM FOR *JOHN B. DOE, ODIG-INV, DCIS, MID-ATLANTIC FIELD*
OFFICE

SUBJECT: Delegation of Authority for the Government Purchase Card Program-Billing Official

References: (a) Federal Acquisition Regulation, Parts 3, 4, 8, and 13 of the FAR
           (b) DoD Financial Management Regulation 7000.14-R, Volumes 4, 5, and 10
           (c) IGDINST 4100.33, *Government Purchase Card Program*

1. You are hereby designated as a Government Purchase Card (GPC) Program Billing Official for the *ODIG-INV, DCIS, Mid-Atlantic Field Office*. You completed the mandatory GPC training program and you are authorized to be assigned Cardholders and Convenience Checkwriters to your billing account. The supplies and services your assigned Cardholders and Convenience Checkwriters procure must be for mission essential OIG requirements. This is supplies and services necessary for OIG employees to perform daily and direct job functions.

2. In executing your GPC responsibilities, you must comply with the applicable laws and regulations, OIG policy, and your delegation of authority, as stated in this memorandum. Responsibilities are listed in the attachment. You are responsible for approving and verifying purchases made by your Cardholders and Convenience Checkwriters. You are pecuniarily liable for purchases you approve. If the violation(s) are serious enough, the result may be civil, administrative, or criminal penalties.

3. Your billing cycle limit is *$180,000*. Your fiscal year limit is *$900,000*. You must not exceed your purchase authority, unless you receive Agency/Organization Program Coordinator (A/OPC) approval. You may not be assigned more than seven Cardholders and/or Convenience Checkwriters to your account. The following Cardholders and Convenience Checkwriter are assigned to your account upon activation:

a. *Name*	Cardholder	Single Limit-*$2,500/$3,000*	Cycle Limit-*$25,000*
b. *Name*	Cardholder	Single Limit-*$2,500/$3,000*	Cycle Limit-*$25,000*
c. *Name*	Cardholder	Single Limit-*$2,500/$3,000*	Cycle Limit-*$30,000*
d. *Name*	Cardholder	Single Limit-*$2,500/$3,000*	Cycle Limit-*$30,000*
e. *Name*	Cardholder	Single Limit-*$2,500/$3,000*	Cycle Limit-*$30,000*
f. *Name*	Cardholder	Single Limit-*$2,500/$3,000*	Cycle Limit-*$30,000*
g. *Name*	Checkwriter	Single Limit-*$2,500/$3,000*	Cycle Limit-*$10,000*

4. You shall comply with your A/OPC's and Component specific procedures to reconcile your account for each billing cycle and complete annual refresher training. In your absence, the

alternate Billing Official for your account is *Amy C. Jones, DCIS-Mid-Atlantic Field Office at (703) 111-1234.*

5. You shall sign the receipt acknowledgement below for your delegation of authority acceptance. Please forward a signed copy to: Department of Defense, Office of Inspector General, 400 Army Navy Drive, Suite 115, ATTN: A/OPC, Arlington, Virginia 22202.

6. This delegation of authority is effective upon account activation. Your delegation of authority is valid until formally modified, suspended, or terminated, and your authority cannot be re-delegated. You must notify your A/OPC prior to separation from the OIG for transferring records and Cardholder and Convenience Checkwriter accounts.

7. If you have questions about your appointment or any other GPC Program questions, please contact the A/OPC, Administration and Logistics Services Directorate at: (703) 604-9836 or fax (703) 604-5006 or *A/OPC email.*

Name
Director
Administration and Logistics
Services Directorate

Attachment: Billing Official Responsibilities

Delegation of Authority to establish a GPC billing account for:

John B. Doe

Billing cycle purchase limit must not exceed *$180,000*
Fiscal year limit must not exceed *$900,000*

I reviewed the IGDINST 4100.33, *GPC Program,* in its entirety, which outlines the OIG policy for adherence to the GPC Program. I acknowledge receipt for the above stated delegation of authority and I accept responsibility for the GPC billing account to be issued in my name.

Printed Name: _____

Signature: _____   Date: _____

Work Telephone: _____

**APPENDIX J (cont'd)
BILLING OFFICIAL RESPONSIBILITIES**

1. If a purchase card or convenience checks are lost, stolen, or fraudulently used/forged, the Billing Official must submit a written report to the A/OPC.

2. The Billing Official shall establish specific account maintenance/reconciliation procedures for each assigned account holder, complete required account reconciliation, and report questionable purchase transaction to his/her supervisor and/or the A/OPC.

3. The Billing Official must comply with applicable laws, regulations, OIG policy, and his/her delegation of authority memorandum in overseeing all assigned Cardholder and Convenience Checkwriter accounts. The Billing Official ensures compliance with program requirements:

  a. Written request and purchase justification.

  b. Required signatures for: Component, Special Authorization (if applicable), and Billing Official approval.

  c. Utilizing existing contracts.

  d. Mandatory sources to include mandatory vendors for office supplies.

  e. Restricted sources.

  f. Prohibited/restricted purchases.

  g. Accountable property reporting.

  h. Tax exempt status.

  i. Split purchases.

  j. Funds availability/certification.

  k. Receiving Official acceptance.

  l. Account reconciliation for all accounts.

  m. Resolving disputes and processing credits.

  n. Certified billing cycle statement (Prompt Payment).

  o. Records retention.

  p. Reviews and audits to include corrective action.

APPENDIX K
PROHIBITED PURCHASES

The following alphabetical listing provides a quick scan of prohibited purchases. The list is not all inclusive and there may be limited exceptions to the general rule. See Chapter 3 for further detail.

A
Alcoholic beverages
Ammunition
Antiques
Ash trays

B
Bonds

C
Carafe sets
Cash advances
China or crystal
Cigars
Classified or controlled cryptographic items
Clothing, personal
Cosmetics
Costumes (Santa suits)
Cutlery, silverware

F
Fuel for personal vehicle
Furniture not in keeping with the office environment; not justified by position/grade level

G
Gambling, casino or horse race betting
Gift Certificates/Cards
Groceries

I
Invitations for a ceremonial/occasion

J
Jewelry

**APPENDIX K (cont'd)
PROHIBITED PURCHASES**

L
Land or building rentals
Leased-vehicle or personal car repairs

M
Memberships fees for professional organizations (personal)
Mementos

P
Party supplies
Personal bills
Personal convenience/preference items
Personal services - paying taxes, court costs, etc.
Pictures not related to your agency's mission

R
Restaurant purchases

S
Salaries, wages, or travel claims
Seasonal decorations
Suitcases, garment bags, duffel bags
Sunglasses

T
Taxidermy services
Telecommunications systems
Tissues, facial
Travel related purchases
Tobacco products

U
Utility services

V
Vehicle expenses for GSA leased vehicles

W
Weapons

APPENDIX L
IG FORM 34-1, GOVERNMENT PURCHASE CARD LOG

GOVERNMENT PURCHASE CARD LOG

Cardholder		For the Billing Cycle ending	
Single Purchase Limit		Billing Cycle Limit	

Instructions: Use this format to document ALL purchases made using the Government Purchase Card. Separate entries are required for each line on the order. The total of all items on an order must not exceed your single purchase limit.

Order Date	Control No.	Vendor's Name Address and Contact	Description	Qty.	Unit of Issue	Unit Price	Total Price	Credit	Card Balance	Account Statement	
										Amount Billed	Accountable (Y or N)

IG FORM 34-1, Jul 2009 (IGDINST 4100.33)   (PREVIOUS EDITIONS ARE OBSOLETE)   AdobeAcrobat 9.0 Pro

APPENDIX M
IG FORM 34-2, GOVERNMENT PURCHASE CARD OR CONVENIENCE CHECK DESTRUCTION CERTIFICATE

DEPARTMENT OF DEFENSE
OFFICE OF INSPECTOR GENERAL
GOVERNMENT PURCHASE CARD or CONVENIENCE CHECK
CERTIFICATE OF DESTRUCTION

☐ I certify the **Government Purchase Card** issued to:

Cardholder Name: _____

Card Number (last four): _____

Destruction Date: _____ *(cut into four pieces)*

☐ I certify the **Government Purchase Convenience Checks** issued to:

Convenience Checkwriter Name: _____

Check Numbers: _____

Destruction Date: _____ *(shredded)*

Billing Official

Print Last Name	First Name Middle	Initial
Component	Location	Work Telephone
Date	Signature	

Witness

Print Last Name	First Name	Middle Initial
Date	Signature	

Note: Forward completed form to the Government Purchase Card Agency/ Organization Program Coordinator and retain a copy in the Billing Official's records.

IG FORM 34-2 JUL 2009 (IGDINST 4100.33) (PREVIOUS EDITIONS ARE OBSOLETE)   AdobeAcrobat 9.0 Pro

APPENDIX N
IG FORM 34-3, GOVERNMENT PURCHASE CARD
REQUEST FOR SUPPLIES AND SERVICES

DEPARTMENT OF DEFENSE / OFFICE OF INSPECTOR GENERAL GOVERNMENT PURCHASE CARD REQUEST FOR SUPPLIES AND SERVICES *(Excluding Training Related Expenses)*		1. CONTROL NUMBER	2. DATE
3. FROM	4. THRU	5. TO	

PART I - LIST SUPPLIES AND SERVICES BELOW *(Continue on plain sheet if necessary)*

6. FOR	7. DELIVERY TO		8. NO LATER THAN

9. Mfg Part or Stock Number	10. Supplies or Services Description	11. Quantity	12. Unit of Issue	13. Estimated Unit Price	14. Estimated Total Cost
					15. Total

16. Suggested Sources: *(Include Phone Number, Address & POC)*

PART II - JUSTIFICATION AND PURPOSE

17. Justification and purpose as related to the primary mission:

PART III - APPROVALS AND REQUIRED SIGNATURES

18. DATE	19. **Requester** *(Print Name, Title & Phone Number)*	20. Signature

I certify the above purchase request is mission essential.

21. DATE	22. **Supervisor or Designee** *(Print Name, Title & Phone Number)*	23. Signature

Special Authorization *(check one)* ☐ Approve ☐ Disapprove

24. DATE	25. **Approving Official** *(Print Name, Title & Phone Number)*	26. Signature

I certify funds are available for this purchase. For an open market source, I certify mandatory sources do not meet mission requirements.

27. DATE	28. **Cardholder/Convenience Checkwriter** *(Print Name & Phone Number)*	29. Signature

Billing Official *(check one)* ☐ Approve ☐ Disapprove

30. DATE	31. **Billing Official** *(Print Name & Phone Number)*	32. Signature
33. DATE	34. **Receiving Official** *(Print Name, Title & Phone Number)*	35. Signature

IG FORM 34-3, JUL 2009 (IGDINST 4100.33) (PREVIOUS EDITIONS ARE OBSOLETE)   AdobeAcrobat 9.0 Pro

APPENDIX N (cont'd)
IG FORM 34-3, GOVERNMENT PURCHASE CARD
REQUEST FOR SUPPLIES AND SERVICES

Instructions for the Government Purchase
Card Request for Supplies and Services
(Excluding Training Related Expenses)
IG Form 34-3

General - Ensure form is thoroughly reviewed and completed prior to signing for approval of purchases.

1. **Control Number:** An internal number assigned by the Cardholder/Convenience Checkwriter.

2. **Date:** Current date, will be automatically filled in.

3. **From:** Requester office symbol/address.

4. **Thru:** Component supervisor or designee office symbol/address.

5. **To:** Component Cardholder/Convenience Checkwriter office symbol/address. All others use "A&M/ALSD".

6. **For:** Name of individual and office.

7. **Deliver To:** Address and room number where the supplies or services are to be delivered.

8. **No Later Than:** The date the supplies or services are needed.

9. **Mfg Part or Stock Number:** Part or stock number assigned to the item from catalog or vendor.

10. **Supplies or Services Description:** Name of the item. Describe the characteristics of the supplies or service.

11. **Quantity:** Number of items required.

12. **Unit of Issue:** How the item is packaged (example: each).

13. **Estimated Unit Price:** Cost per item.

14. **Estimated Total Cost:** Total cost for each line item.

15. **Total:** Total dollar amount of the order.

IG FORM 34-3 , (Instructions) JUL 2009

APPENDIX N (cont'd)
IG FORM 34-3, GOVERNMENT PURCHASE CARD
REQUEST FOR SUPPLIES AND SERVICES

16. Suggested Sources: Name of vendor, address, point of contact, and phone number. DoD EMall or GSA Advantage are mandatory sources/schedules for procurements, unless, a lower price for an identical item (same make and model) is available from another source (open market). Purchasing from DoD EMall or GSA Advantage takes priority over an open market source with consideration to availability, delivery costs, and shipping time.

17. Justification and Purpose: The purpose for the supply or service, as related to the primary mission.

18-20. Requester: The current date, typed name, title, phone number, and signature of the Requester.

21-23. Supervisor or Designee: The current date, typed name, title, phone number, and signature of the Supervisor or Designee.

24-26. Approving Official: The current date, typed name, title, phone number and signature of the Approving Official for special authorization.
"Special authorization is required for: shredders, special drinking water, office furnishings, such as furniture, window treatments, and carpet, accountable property, reproduction equipment, information technology and telecommunications equipment."

27-29. Cardholder/Convenience Checkwriter: The current date, typed name, phone number, and signature of the Cardholder/Convenience Checkwriter for fund certification.

30-32. Billing Official: The current date, typed name, phone number, and signature of the Billing Official for purchase approval.

33-35. Receiving Official: The current date, typed name, title, phone number, and signature of the Receiving Official for receipt acceptance.

IG FORM 34-3 , (Instructions (cont.))

APPENDIX O
IG FORM 34-4, CARDHOLDER/CONVENIENCE CHECKWRITER
REQUEST/CHANGE APPOINTMENT

**DEPARTMENT OF DEFENSE
OFFICE OF INSPECTOR GENERAL**

GOVERNMENT PURCHASE CARD (GPC)
CARDHOLDER/CONVENIENCE CHECKWRITER
REQUEST/CHANGE APPOINTMENT

COMPONENT
- [ ] Administration and Management
- [ ] Administrative Investigations
- [ ] Audit
- [ ] Intelligence
- [ ] Investigations
- [ ] Policy and Oversight
- [ ] Other _____

APPOINTMENT TYPE:
- [ ] Cardholder or
- [ ] Convenience Checkwriter

ACTION REQUESTED
- [ ] Appointment
- [ ] Termination
- [ ] Change
  - [ ] Transfer to a New Billing Official
  - [ ] Change Purchase Limit
  - [ ] Change of Address
  - [ ] Other _____

RECOMMENDED APPOINTEE'S INFORMATION

1a. Last Name	1b. First Name	1c. Middle Initial	2a. Work Mailing Address: *Street Address or Box Number (include suite, room, or floor as appropriate)*
2b. City	2c. State	2d. Zip Code	
3. Work Phone Number	4. Work Cell Phone		5. FAX
6. Work E-mail Address	7a. Single Purchase Limit		7b. Billing Limit

8. Required Training: *Attach Certificates (must be current-within 6 months)*	a. GPC Course CLG001- (Defense Acquisition University) Date Completed _____	b. Ethics Training (OIG Intranet) Date Completed: _____

BILLING OFFICIAL INFORMATION

1a. Last Name	1b. First Name	1c. Middle Initial

2. List all current GPC Cardholders and/or Convenience Checkwriters assigned to your Billing Official account, below.

(1)	(2)
(3)	(4)

(5)	(6)	(7)

3. Billing Official Signature:	4. Date

COMPONENT HEAD OR DESIGNEE [ ] Approve [ ] Disapprove

1a. Last Name	1b. First Name	1c. Middle Initial	2. Title
3. Signature:			4. Date

IG Form 34-4, JUL 2009 (IGDINST 4100.33)   AdobeAcrobat 9.0 Pro

APPENDIX P
IG FORM 34-5, GOVERNMENT PURCHASE CARD
BILLING OFFICIAL REQUEST/CHANGE APPOINTMENT

DEPARTMENT OF DEFENSE
OFFICE OF INSPECTOR GENERAL

GOVERNMENT PURCHASE CARD (GPC)
BILLING OFFICIAL
REQUEST/CHANGE APPOINTMENT

COMPONENT	ACTION REQUESTED
☐ Administration and Management	☐ Appointment
☐ Administrative Investigations	☐ Primary
☐ Audit	☐ Alternate
☐ Intelligence	☐ Termination
☐ Investigations	☐ Change
☐ Policy and Oversight	☐ Purchase Limit
☐ Other _____	☐ Address
	☐ Other _____

BILLING OFFICIAL'S INFORMATION

1a. Last Name	1b. First Name	1c. Middle Initial	2a. Work Mailing Address: *Street Address or Box Number (include suite, room, or floor as appropriate)*
2b. City	2c. State	2d. Zip Code	
3. Work Phone Number	4. Work Cell Phone		5. FAX
6. Work E-mail Address	7a. Yearly Limit		7b. Billing Cycle Limit
Required Training: *Attach Certificates (must be current-within 6 months)*	9. GPC Course CLG001- (Defense Acquisition University) Date Completed _____		10. Ethics Training (OIG Intranet) Date Completed: _____

11. List all current GPC Cardholders and/or Convenience Checkwriters assigned to your Billing Official account.

(1)	(2)
(3)	(4)
(5)	(6)	(7)

COMPONENT HEAD OR DESIGNEE ☐ Approval ☐ Disapprove

1a. Last Name	1b. First Name	1c. Middle Initial	2. Title
3. Signature			4. Date

IG Form 34-5, JUL 2009 (IGDINST 4100.33)   AdobeAcrobat 9.0 Pro

APPENDIX Q
DD FORM 577, APPOINTMENT/TERMINATION
RECORD – AUTHORIZED SIGNATURE

APPOINTMENT/TERMINATION RECORD - AUTHORIZED SIGNATURE
(Read Privacy Act Statement and Instructions before completing form.)

PRIVACY ACT STATEMENT

AUTHORITY: E.O. 9397, 31 U.S.C. §§ 3325, 3528, DoD Financial Management Regulation, Vol. 5, Chapter 33, and DoDD 7000.15, DoD Accountable Officials and Certifying Officers.
PRINCIPAL PURPOSE(S): To maintain a record of certifying and accountable officers' appointments, and termination of those appointments. The information will also be used for identification purposes associated with certification of documents and/or liability of public records and funds.
ROUTINE USE(S): The information on this form may be disclosed as generally permitted under 5 U.S.C. § 552a(b) of the Privacy Act of 1974, as amended. It may also be disclosed outside of the Department of Defense (DoD) to the the Federal Reserve banks to verify authority of the accountable individual to issue Treasury checks. In addition, other Federal, State and local government agencies, which have identified a need to know, may obtain this information for the purpose(s) identified in the DoD Blanket Routine Uses published in the Federal Register.
DISCLOSURE: Voluntary; however, failure to provide the requested information may preclude appointment.

SECTION I - FROM: COMMANDER/APPOINTING AUTHORITY

1. NAME *(First, Middle Initial, Last)*	2. TITLE	3. DOD COMPONENT/ORGANIZATION
4. DATE *(YYYYMMDD)*	5. SIGNATURE	

SECTION II - TO: APPOINTEE

6. NAME *(First, Middle Initial, Last)*	7. SSN	8. TITLE
9. DOD COMPONENT/ORGANIZATION	10. ADDRESS *(Include ZIP Code)*	
11. TELEPHONE NUMBER *(Include Area Code)*	12. EFFECTIVE DATE OF APPOINTMENT *(YYYYMMDD)*	

13. POSITION TO WHICH APPOINTED *(X one)*

	CERTIFYING OFFICER		ACCOUNTABLE OFFICIAL		OTHER *(Specify)*

14. YOU ARE HEREBY APPOINTED TO SERVE IN THE CAPACITY SHOWN ABOVE. YOUR RESPONSIBILITIES WILL INCLUDE:

15. YOU ARE ADVISED TO REVIEW AND ADHERE TO THE FOLLOWING REGULATION(S) NEEDED TO ADEQUATELY PERFORM THE DUTIES TO WHICH YOU HAVE BEEN ASSIGNED:

DoDFMR, Vol. 5, chapter 33;

SECTION III - ACKNOWLEDGEMENT OF APPOINTMENT

I acknowledge and accept the position and responsibilities defined above. I understand that I am strictly liable to the United States for all public funds under my control. I have been counseled on my pecuniary liability and have been given written operating instructions. I certify that my official signature is shown in the box below.

16. PRINTED NAME *(First, Middle Initial, Last)*	17. SIGNATURE

SECTION IV - TERMINATION OF APPOINTMENT

	The appointment of the individual named above is hereby revoked.	18. EFFECTIVE DATE *(YYYYMMDD)*	19. APPOINTEE INITIALS
20. NAME OF COMMANDER/APPOINTING AUTHORITY	21. TITLE	22. SIGNATURE	

DD FORM 577, JAN 2004   PREVIOUS EDITIONS ARE OBSOLETE.   Adobe Professional 7.0

APPENDIX R
SF 182, AUTHORIZATION, AGREEMENT AND CERTIFICATION OF TRAINING

AUTHORIZATION, AGREEMENT AND CERTIFICATION OF TRAINING	A. Agency, code agency subelement and submitting office number	B. Request Status (Mark (X) one) ☐ Resubmission ☐ Initial ☐ Correction ☐ Cancellation

Section A - TRAINEE INFORMATION
Please read instructions on page 6 before completing this form

1. Applicant's Name (Last, First, Middle Initial)	2. Social Security Number/Federal Employee Number	3. Date of Birth (yyyy-mm-dd)

4. Home Address (Number, Street, City, State, ZIP Code) (Optional)	5. Home Telephone (Optional) (include Area Code)	6. Position Level (Mark (X) one) ☐ a. Non-supervisory ☐ b. Manager ☐ c. Supervisory ☐ d. Executive

7. Organization Mailing Address (Branch-Division/Office/Bureau/Agency)	8. Office Telephone (Include Area Code and Extension)	9. Work Email Address

10. Position Title	11. Does applicant need special accomodation? ☐ Yes ☐ No	If yes, please describe below

12. Type of Appointment	13. Education Level (click link to view codes or go to page 7)	14. Pay Plan	15. Series	16. Grade	17. Step

Section B - TRAINING COURSE DATA

1a. Name and Mailing Address of Training Vendor (No., Street, City, State, ZIP Code)	1b. Location of Training Site (if same, mark box) ☐
	1c. Vendor Telephone Number / 1d. Vendor Email Address

2a. Course Title	2b. Course Number Code	3. Training Start Date (Enter Date as yyyy-mm-dd)	4. Training End Date (Enter Date as yyyy-mm-dd)

5. Training Duty Hours	6. Training Non-Duty Hours	7. Training Purpose Type (Click link to view codes or go to page 9)	8. Training Type Code (Click link to view codes or go to page 9)

9. Training Sub Type Code (Click link to view codes or go to page 9)	10. Training Delivery Type Code (Click link to view codes or go to page 12)	11. Training Designation Type Code (Click link to view codes or go to page 13)	12. Training Credit	13. Training Credit Type Code (Click link to view codes or go to page 13)

14. Training Accreditation Indicator (Check below) ☐ Yes ☐ No	15. Continued Service Agreement Required Indicator (Check below) ☐ Yes ☐ No ☐ N/A	16. Continued Service Agreement Expiration Date (Enter date as yyyy-mm-dd)	17. Training Source Type Code (Click link to view codes or go to page 13)

18. Training Objective	19. AGENCY USE ONLY

Section C - COSTS AND BILLING INFORMATION

1. Direct Costs and Appropriation / Fund Chargeable			2. Indirect Costs and Appropriation / Fund Chargeable		
Item	Amount	Appropriation Fund	Item	Amount	Appropriation Fund
a. Tuition and Fees	$		a. Travel	$	
b. Books & Material Costs	$		b. Per Diem	$	
c. TOTAL	$		c. TOTAL	$	

3. Total Training Non-Government Contribution Cost	6. BILLING INSTRUCTIONS (Furnish invoice to:)
4. Document / Purchasing Order / Requisition Number	
5. 8 - Digit Station Symbol (Example - 12-34-5678)	

U.S. Office of Personnel Management

Standard Form 182
Revised December 2006
All previous editions not usable.

APPENDIX R (cont'd)

Section D - APPROVALS	
1a. Immediate Supervisor - *Name and title*	
1b. Area Code / Telephone Number	1c. Email Address
1d. Signature	1e. Date
2a. Second-line Supervisor - *Name and title*	
2b. Area Code / Telephone Number	2c. Email Address
2d. Signature	2e. Date
3a Training Officer - *Name and title*	
3b. Area Code / Telephone Number	3c. Email Address
3d. Signature	3e. Date

Section E - APPROVALS / CONCURRENCE	
1a. Authorizing Official - *Name and title*	
1b. Area Code / Telephone Number	1c. Email Address
1d. Signature ☐ Approved ☐ Disapproved	1e. Date

Section F - CERTIFICATION OF TRAINING COMPLETION AND EVALUATION	
1a. Authorizing Official - *Name and title*	
1b. Area Code / Telephone Number	1c. Email Address
1d. Signature	1e. Date

TRAINING FACILITY ~ Bills should be sent to office indicated in item C6. ı Please refer to number given in item C4 to assure prompt payment.

U.S. Office of Personnel Management   Page 2   Standard Form 182
Revised December 2006
All previous editions not usable.